T0288808

CRIMEA

NEIL KENT

Crimea

A History

HURST & COMPANY, LONDON

First published in the United Kingdom in 2016 by
C. Hurst & Co. (Publishers) Ltd.,
41 Great Russell Street, London, WC1B 3PL
© Neil Kent, 2016
All rights reserved.
Printed in the United States of America

Distributed in the United States, Canada and Latin America by
Oxford University Press, 198 Madison Avenue, New York, NY 10016,
United States of America.

The right of Neil Kent to be identified as the author
of this publication is asserted by him in accordance with the
Copyright, Designs and Patents Act, 1988.

A Cataloguing-in-Publication data record for this book
is available from the British Library.

978-1-84904-463-9 *hardback*

This book is printed using paper from registered sustainable
and managed sources.

www.hurstpublishers.com

CONTENTS

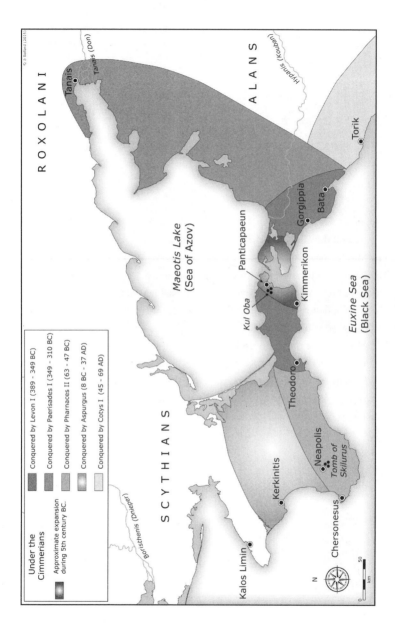

Ancient Greek Crimea

Legend:

Under the Cimmerians

- Conquered by Levon I (389 - 349 BC)
- Conquered by Paerisades I (349 - 310 BC)
- Conquered by Pharnaces II (63 - 47 BC)
- Conquered by Aspurgus (8 BC - 37 AD)
- Conquered by Cotys I (45 - 69 AD)

Approximate expansion during 5th century BC.

ROXOLANI

SCYTHIANS

ALANS

Maeotis Lake (Sea of Azov)

Euxine Sea (Black Sea)

Tanais

Tanais (Don)

Hypanis (Kouban)

Torik

Bata

Gorgippia

Kimmerikon

Panticapaeun

Kul Oba

Theodoro

Neapolis

Tomb of Skilurus

Kerkinitis

Chersonesus

Kalos Limin

Borysthenis (Dnieper)

N

© J. Ballard c2015

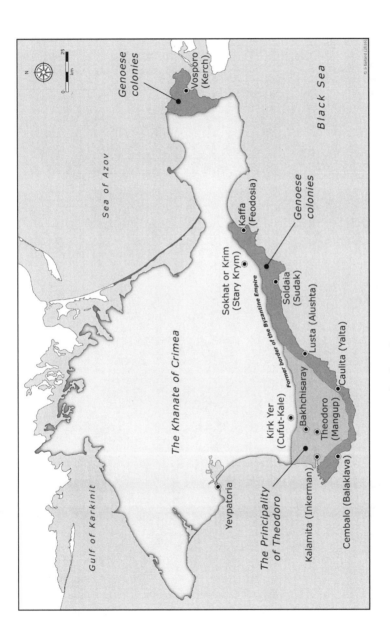

Mid-Fifteenth Century Crimea

Crimean War

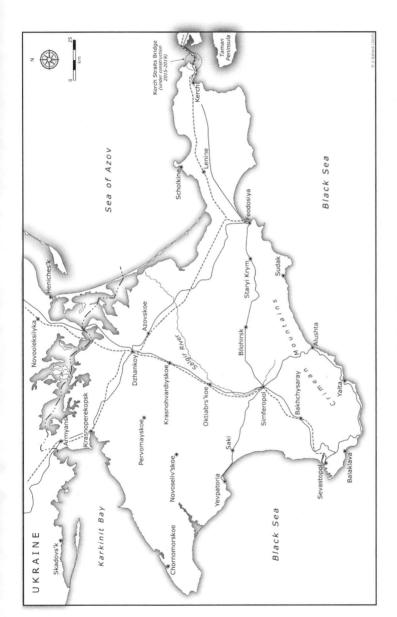

Modern Crimea

INTRODUCTION

When, in 2006, I made my first visit to Ukraine, my key destination was Crimea and I undertook the long journey by car from Kiev to the northern border, a distance of some 675 kilometres, at a leisurely pace. On the way, I visited the towns and countryside with which I had long become familiar from the Russian literature of nineteenth century authors such as Nikolai Gogol and Anton Chekhov. Yet what struck me particularly as I crossed the great southern steppes which spread out for thousands of kilometres, was the appearance of many of the roads leading south to Crimea. They were lined with beautiful avenues of deciduous trees much like the alleys to stately homes throughout Europe. It then became clear to me that this eastern part of Europe, for all the monotony and exoticness of the steppes, was in reality no wild and alien land. Rather, in terms of appearance, it was part and parcel of the European landscape and its peoples and culture were European, not Asiatic, even if over a millennium ago many of those who had settled here had come from far to the east.

For steppe areas to the north and west, Crimea was the gateway to Europe and therefore perhaps even more significant for Russia than St Petersburg hundreds of years later. It was from here, a millennium ago that farming and animal husbandry, as cattle raising, was introduced, and, in reverse, slaves exported.

For me on my first visit, the first significant site I met with just north of the land entrance to Crimea was a settlement of immense historic and cultural fascination – Zaporozhye – not in Crimea proper but actually on the River Dnieper, in south-eastern Ukraine, 221 kilometres from the border of Crimea. It was built in 1775 and, until 1921, was known as Alexandrovsk, the site of an important fortress on the left bank guarding Russia and its newly won southern territories against the depredations of the Crimean Tatars, nominal vassals of the Ottoman Turks, to the south. They were – and in some senses remained for centuries – sworn enemies of imperialistic Russia. Yet the town is of interest for other reasons, in particular, as the site of the Zaporozhian Sich, an old Cossack military settlement and now the location of a highly important museum dedicated to the culture and history of the Zaporozhian Cossacks. Situated on the northern half of the rugged Khotritsa Island, that stands in the middle of the River Dnieper, which previously defended it like a moat, this unusual museum offers the visitor a wealth of information related to the Zaporozhian Cossacks. A free people, unencumbered by the feudal ties which prevailed in the early modern period throughout much of central and eastern Europe, they were a highly war-like ethnos, whose spartan lifestyle and aggressiveness proved invaluable when harnessed to the service of the Russian tsar in his battles, not only against Tatars and Ottoman Turks, but the Poles and Austrians as well. Their military camp on the island had been a bastion of Orthodox Russian authority for two centuries, keeping the Islamic Khanate of the Crimean Tatars to the south at bay, until 1775, when the Russian Empress Catherine the Great no longer needed its defensive services: by this time, much of the former Tatar territories north of Crimea had been successfully conquered by Russia and in 1783 Crimea itself was annexed to the southern part of today's Ukraine – then Novorossiya (New Russia). With the purpose of acting as a stepping stone south, to Constantinople itself, which imperial Russia of the eighteenth century so ardently hoped to absorb into its political and spiritual fold.

Geography

The unique situation of Crimea at the geographical crossroads of Eurasia continues to define its identity. This south-eastern part of the Eurasian landmass, of which Crimea is a part, assumed its present shape some eight thousand years ago towards the end of the last ice age and it encompasses a vast range of geographical regions stretching from the Carpathian Mountains in the west – much of which is now under Ukrainian and Romanian sovereignty – to the increasingly arid steppes of the east which, under Russia and Ukraine, reach towards what are today the central Asian republics and Mongolia. Indeed, the peninsula of Crimea itself, although only relatively small by contrast – at some 24,900 square kilometres, it is, the size of Maryland in the United States or just under double the size of Yorkshire, in England – possesses strikingly distinct geographical regions. These include the lowland steppes of the north, which cover two thirds of Crimea, the rugged and forbidding interior mountains, and the often lush and stunningly beautiful southern coastline, which, more than anything resembles the French Riviera – not only in its appearance but also in terms of its unusually balmy climate, which so contrasts with the windswept and brutally cold, steppes of the north.

Situated on the north-eastern coast of the Black Sea, Crimea is joined in the north to the rest of the Eurasian land mass by the Isthmus of Perekop, to the east of which lies the Sea of Azov. Today two important roads give access to Crimea, one in the north-west heading south from Armyansk, the other in the north-east from Henichesk. However, in former times it was the sea routes that were of greater importance. The Kerch peninsula which points to the narrow (at most only 13 kilometres) Straits of Kerch to the east almost abuts the Russian mainland and, since the disputed reunion of Crimea to Russia in 2014. It had originally been annexed by Russia in 1783 but in 1954 it was ceded to Ukraine. A linking bridge has been promised, which will compensate for the troubled land border which now exists to the north.

The Sea

Today, transport communications are largely overland, but historically it was the fact that the Strait of Kerch linked the Sea of Azov in the north-east to the Black Sea in the south, which was of greater importance for human migrations and maritime trade, linking the entire Black Sea littoral not only to the Mediterranean world to the south, but also to the vast and rich territories of the Eurasian interior. As such, the sea is an integral part of the Crimean landscape and has long been depicted in the paintings which have made the region's geographical beauty world famous, not least in the maritime themes of the nineteenth-century Ukrainian artist Arkhyp Kuindzhi (c.1842–1910), from nearby Mariupol, who had studied at the Russian Imperial Academy of Art, in St Petersburg and whose famous works adorn the walls of the Russian Museum there.

Yet the seas around Crimea are fascinating for other reasons. The depths of the Black Sea hide an extraordinary secret from the overwhelming majority of people who have come to these shores: just below the 90-metre depth of the salt-rich upper layer, in which fish abound, there is another layer of water worthy of Greek mythology for its symbolism. Here no living creature can survive, although once they did. With the advent of the fresh waters which poured in from the melting ice cap to the north during the last Ice Age, its vegetation proceeded to decompose, emitting a noxious gas containing hydrogen sulphide which wiped out all forms of life in these depths. Occasionally it erupts onto the surface the gases shimmering purple and more rarely still even bursts into flames.

But my own transport to Crimea was not maritime but automotive and as I drove south into Crimea taking the eastern route (E105), I was struck by the aridity of the northern swathe of the peninsula, mainly formed by steppes similar to those characterising the land to the north of the isthmus, the homeland of the Cossacks. They appeared sparsely inhabited with few trees and their resemblance to the prairie lands of the American Midwest was striking. Dzankoi (its Tatar name signifies that it was a 'new' town) is its only significant city is highly industrialised and has a population of only 36,000 people. During the early Soviet period, many Jews had lived in the vicinity working on collective farms, but during the Nazi occupation in the Second World War (known as the Great Patriotic War, in the former Soviet Union) it was the site of a Jewish concentration camp, where many Jews lost their lives.

Mountainous Southern Interior

Further south lies a wide swathe of mountains which serve to protect the lush southern coastal area from some of the worst effects of the harsh Russian winter. These are the Crimean Mountains – three parallel ranges running from coast to coast. Although not very high when compared to those of the Carpathians, Urals or Caucasus which define the borders of this part of the Eurasian landmass, they do rise to considerable heights: the peaks of Roman-Kosh (1,545 metres) and Chatyr-Dag (1,527 metres) are amongst the highest, but Ai-Petri (1,234 metres) is the most famous, as it is so close to Yalta, on the southern coast. As a consequence, while temperatures plunge to well below freezing in Dzankoi, in Yalta, which is sheltered by the cliff-like southern range of Yaila, they tend to remain several degrees above. This has allowed a Russian Riviera to develop over the last couple of centuries, on which first Russian royalty and aristocrats, then the growing Russian middle classes and finally Soviet workers, were able to enjoy the seaside pleasures and lush flora of its environs. Vineyards thrived here for millennia and reached their zenith in terms of quality under the watchful eye of imperial viniculturists who made the imperial wine estate Massandra – with its imposing palace, a summer home to the tsar and his family – a byword for high quality Muscat dessert wines. The estate was first established by the Polish Count Potocki in 1783, but was transferred in the middle of the following century to Count Mikhail Vorontsov, governor of New Russia and military leader of Russian campaigns in the Caucasus. In 1889 it was acquired by Tsar Alexander III and remained an imperial property until the fall of the Romanovs in 1917. Sweet wines and liquors are still produced there today, albeit for a less discerning palette than those of their imperial majesties when Prince Lev Galitzen managed the vinery of the estate. Along with Muscat and Pinot Gris, such local varieties as Ekim-Kara, Kethessia, Capita-n-Kara, Lapa-Kara and Metin-Kara are grown, a litany of names clearly Crimean Turkic in origin.

The Russian Riviera

The narrow coastal region of this Russian Riviera, centred on Yalta, stretches for some 150 kilometres, but is only 2 to 12 kilometres wide, it contains a plethora of ancient towns including Yevpatoria, home of the Judaised Karaite Tatars; Sevastopol (seat of Russia's Black Sea Fleet); Sudak (with its ancient, darkly looming, picturesque fortress), Feodosia (ancient mercantile centre for wheat and slaves) and Kerch (fortress town and gateway to Russia across the straits).

Ancient Prehistoric Heritage

The Russian imperial period of the nineteenth and early twentieth centuries was doubtless the architectural and cultural heyday of Crimea in terms of art, architecture and literature, but it should not be forgotten that human ancestors have lived there as far back as the Middle Paleolithic Period, some 80,000 years ago. However, the bones that have been found are from extinct Neanderthal peoples – now said to be some of the ancestors of many non-African humans today – not the Cro-Magnon who are our own immediate relatives. Uncovered in 1924 in the cave of Kiyik-Koba 25 kilometres east of Simferopol, by Russian archaeologist Gleb Bonch-Osmolovsky, they are the first evidence of human remains in the peninsula from such an early date. He excavated different cultural levels, uncovering flint tools and the bones of various animals, including those of the long extinct mammoths and woolly rhinoceros. These Neanderthal people lived by hunting and gathering and they buried their dead, as the discovery of graves in the caves demonstrates. Other, later Neanderthal remains, from about 30,000 years ago, have also been uncovered from the rock shelters at Buran Kaya III, not far from Kiyik-Koba. Despite the fact that from some 110,000 years ago until about 12,000 years ago the whole of northern Europe endured an Ice Age which covered the region in deep glaciers, the eastern European steppes and Crimea itself remained free of glaciers and therefore offered settlement opportunities: first for Neanderthal peoples and then Cro-Magnon man.

Already though, from the Late Paleolithic Period, about 40,000 years ago, it would seem that these Neanderthal peoples were increasingly supplanted by modern Cro-Magnon humans, with whom they were, to some unquantifiable degree, interbreeding. Fishing now also seems to have become an important way of acquiring food, supplementing hunting and gathering. The tools used by these peoples were by now more sophisticated than those from earlier epochs and were made not only of flint, but of bone, horn and ivory, probably obtained through barter from huge distances. Artistic expression now comes to the fore for the first time in Crimea, as evinced by the decoration on tools, the decoration of jewellery, shell pendants, ivory bracelets and figurines which often represent both human and animal forms. Furthermore, modern archaeological excavation has uncovered the first Crimean examples of musical instruments, including simple flutes and drums.

The climate of the region seems to have improved about 16,000 years ago, leading to an ever more dense population settlement. Crimea, however, was at this stage not a peninsula but an integral part of the eastern European land mass, only assuming its current geographical appearance in the sixth millennium BC, as the Black Sea rose. Little is known of the inhabitants of this period, but archaeological remains from the Ardych-Burun site have demonstrated that by the middle of the fourth millennium BC tool technology was developing, pottery had come into use and agriculture was now carried out. Indeed, archaeological remains confirm that the inhabitants of Crimea in this period were cultivating wheat and had domesticated pigs.

By the third millennium BC, about the time of the establishment of the First Pharaonic dynasty of Egypt, Crimea is thought to have been settled by Proto-Indo-European speaking peoples. Indeed, first the Cimmerians and then the Scythians made their home in Crimea. Many of the archaeological remains of this period have been preserved underwater off the Crimean coast in the poisonous depths.

INTRODUCTION

Crimean Population Today

According to estimates of the Ukrainian Ministry of Foreign Affairs, who took the last official census before the current political upheavals, the population of Crimea today stands at about 2,018,400. Of these about 1,265,900 are urban and 752,500 rural. Approximately 63 per cent consider themselves ethnic Russians, 25 per cent Ukrainian and about 9 per cent Tatar, although these figures are a matter of contention in the current crisis, and do not reflect those who have left the region as refugees, whether to Ukraine, Russia or elsewhere. In any case, though, Crimea and its multiplicity of peoples over the millennia continues to fascinate the wider world. It has appeared again and again in world literature, including the writings of the late British author and artist Beryl Bainbridge. She took it as the theme of her novel *Master George*, published in 1994, which focuses on its eponymous hero, one George Hardy, a bisexual English surgeon and amateur photographer from Liverpool who travels out to Sevastopol in 1854 as the Crimean War erupts. This war continues to fascinate many people throughout the world today because of the exoticness of its location and the unflinching heroism, in the face of death and adversity, of those on both sides who fought in it. An understanding of Crimea's long history is a necessity in today's world in order to comprehend what binds and divides Europe in political, cultural and social terms, at a time when ancient divisions threaten the very fabric of a common European civilisation, also threatened by external alien forces, as the Mongols threatened the gates of Feodosia (Kaffa) many hundreds of years before.

1

CRIMEA AND THE CLASSICAL WORLD

From its earliest days, Crimea was integrated by trade, migration and cultural exchange with the rest of the Black Sea, Aegean and Mediterranean littorals. Even the shortest visit to its coastal towns and environs gives evidence that Crimea was an integral part of the classical world, by virtue of art, architecture and other artefacts. Today these grace not only its towns, countryside and numerous museums, but the great treasure houses of the world, notably the Hermitage Museum in St Petersburg, Tretyakov Gallery in Moscow, Louvre Museum in Paris and British Museum in London. Their stylistic variations show the diversity of the peoples who settled in Crimea over the millennia, each with their own spiritual beliefs and cultures, forming a symbiosis over the centuries of immense richness, yet each ready to absorb yet further impulses from the latest wave of new settlers.

Cimmerians

The earliest settlers of Crimea in the classical period were the Cimmerians, whose first Greek appearance was in Homer's Odyssey in the eighth century, as well as in the Histories of Herodotus, three centuries later. Herodotus had visited Crimea, rather than merely writing about it at a distance. Yet, for all that, neither historian can be relied on for historical accuracy, if the eighteenth-century French philosopher Voltaire is to be believed. He went as far as to maintain that rather than calling Herodotus 'the Father of History', he should be called 'the Father of Lies', because of his gross inaccuracies and obfuscations. However justified that judgement may be, Herodotus did bring an awareness of Crimea and the peoples who inhabited it in classical times to a wider literary world. In fact, he noted the arrival there of the Cimmerians. These were among the first migratory

waves of Indo-European speaking peoples to arrive in Crimea, having been driven southwards and westwards across the Eurasian steppes in the seventh century BC, by the Scythians, an Iranian people, of Indo-European origin.

A hierarchical ethnos, Cimmerian society maintained a sharp division between the ruling nobility and the common people over whom they ruled, yet they possessed a strong, pride-infused, common identity as a people. For that reason, Herodotus maintained, many Cimmerians committed mass suicide when the Scythians eventually overwhelmed them, those few who survived having then migrated eastwards into Asia. Whether this actually happened, however, is a mystery, which the scant archaeological remains neither confirm nor deny. Indeed, the very existence of the Cimmerians as a specific people with their own cultural and political identity is still debated, as many modern historians and archaeologists consider them really to be a sub-group of the Scythians, other sub-groups of whom followed on their heels.

Scythians

The Scythians, an Indo-Iranian speaking people, arrived in what is now western Ukraine and Crimea from the east in various waves during the eighth and seventh centuries BC. They were able to displace the Cimmerians through their consummate skills as equestrian archers, skills which the Cimmerians did not profess to such a degree. This gave them a huge advantage and so they came to dominate not only Crimea, but much of the Middle East, including Syria, Judaea and western Persia. The great Babylonian city of Nineveh was captured by them in 612 BC. For that reason, they were often in major conflict with the Persians, another Iranian speaking people to the east during their centuries of regional hegemony. Eventually, the Median kings of Persia were successful in wresting western Anatolia from their control, later pushing them back into the Caucasus and beyond. Nonetheless, the invasion by the Persian King Darius the Great and his armies, in 513 BC, was successfully repelled by the Scythians. In consequence, their armies were feared and respected, achieving further renown because they were made up of free soldiers whose only reward was the booty of their enemies whom they had conquered.

Similarly, the Scythians were pitted against the Greek city states to the west, but at a disadvantage in the sense that they had no literary culture of their own. That said, Scythian soldiers adopted many characteristics of the Greeks and are said to have worn Greek-style bronze helmets and chain mail body armour. However, their swords were based on Persian prototypes and they used highly specific double curved bows and trefoil arrows. What gave them their greatest advantage, though, were their horses (generally Mongolian ponies greater in number than the men), which collectively made them the greatest equestrian warriors of their age and in Greek mythology they are justly famous as such. Some of their women were deemed to be incredibly skilled at horsemanship and became renowned as warriors, going down in history as the fearsome Amazons, of which the Roman sculpture after Phidias, the Wounded Amazon, at the Capitoline Museum in Rome, is a striking representation.

The Scythians reached their political zenith in the fifth century BC, much like the Greeks. At the same time they were highly active in trade, dealing not only in such northern commodities as slaves, furs and grain, but also in cattle, honey and wax. Fish was also important, as well as wine, olive oil and luxury goods from the southern climes of the Mediterranean world. This brought them great riches and bolstered their highly hierarchical society in which the nobility dominated, ruled over by a patrilineal hereditary king. Herodotus tells us that this royal house eventually intermarried with Greek royal families. For that reason their graves have proven to be rich troves of splendid archaeological artefacts and precious jewellery. In particular, they were famed for their lavishly decorated metalwork, of which the magnificent solid gold jewellery at the Hermitage Museum in St Petersburg, excavated from the seventeenth to the nineteenth centuries, is the most sublime example. (They are of such rarity that a special ticket is required to view them.) Those uncovered at Kul Oba, near Kerch, in Crimea, that date from the fourth century, are among the most interesting examples. Their stylised animal forms, with images of stags to various degrees recumbent, are aesthetically astounding. Yet, for all their artistic sensitivities, the Scythians were also a highly practical people. It has been said that they were the first ethnic group to wear trousers, which was useful for equestrians and facilitated good horsemanship in battle. Less appealing to modern sensibilities was their religious custom of offering human sacrifice from amongst the relics of a deceased's own household.

Scythian kings were often renowned for their military prowess, in particular, King Ateas who fought against King Philip II of Macedonia in 339BC, a battle in which he fell – perhaps not surprisingly since he was said to be ninety at the time. By now though, the Scythians were in sharp decline, their last known monarch was Palakus, who resided at his capital Neapolis (renamed Simferopol in Russian times and still its administrative capital), until its destruction as a political entity in the second century BC.

The Greek Colonies in Crimea

The Greek presence in Crimea established itself early in the classical period. Indeed, by the sixth century BC they had firmly established their coastal colonies at Chersonesus, the romantic ruins of which are still on view today, Theodoro (Mangup) and Panticapaeum (also known as Bospor). As such they were part of a network of colonies which stretched from Sicily and the coast of southern Italy in the west, to the eastern shores of the Black Sea. During these early years each retained its own cultural identity and political autonomy much as in Greece proper with respect to the fiercely independent Greek city states, in particular, Megara and Miletus. However, the increasing need to assert a united front against the other non-Greek peoples of Crimea led them increasingly to ally themselves with each other, so that by 480 BC Panticapaeum, originally founded as far back 2,600 BC by non-Greek peoples, assumed the overall leadership. In the following century, King Levon I extended its hegemony during his long reign (389– 348 BC) to include not only the Kerch Peninsula in the east of Crimea but the Taman Peninsula as well, on the opposite side of the Straits of Kerch. Its political self-sufficiency was made possible by the wealth brought by the grain trade from the north, the local viniculture, and other enterprises, such as metalwork and fishing. However, Panticapaeum gradually weakened under the increasing pressure of new arrivals from the north and east, as well as the strengthening of its neighbours. Finally, in 110 BC, it was conquered by King Mithradates VI Eupator (the latter epithet signifies that he was born of a noble father) who consolidated his authority over Pontus, the kingdom over which he reigned for so long in the early second century

BC and whose political centre of gravity was across the Straits of Kerch. Towards the end of his long reign, Pontus itself, in turn, fell increasingly subject to the far off authority of Rome, now a force to be reckoned with throughout the known world. In the following years, indeed, the whole of the Black Sea littoral became subject to it. That said, in the non-political sphere, the Greek aspects of its cityscape and culture persisted. This can be seen in the Greek-style acropolis and theatre overlooking the sea that was constructed in Panticapeum in the middle of the third century BC, the ruins of which delight visitors to this day. Moreover, even after its acquisition by Rome, the Mithradatan dynasty continued to retain a modicum of its own authority. Mithradates VI Eupator's granddaughter, Dynamis, was appointed its first queen, reigning from 44–14 BC, over what was now known as the Bosporus Kingdom, but was a territory fully subject to Rome, along with the other formerly independent Greek city states of Crimea.

Taurians

Another people who came to settle in Crimea were the Taurians who, in the classical period, as well as again centuries later, would give their name Taurida (also Tauris) to the region, when it was annexed by Russia in 1783. The name itself is said to signify a mountain people and the root element of Taur is related to the French word 'tour' and our own word 'tower'. The Taurians favoured the mountainous south-east and coastal littoral of the peninsula, at Sybolon (later Balaklava) for settlement. From here they roamed the Black Sea as pirates and Herodotus stated that they lived 'by plundering and war'. They also sacrificed humans to a virgin goddess which, in Greek mythology, inspired the famous tragedy 'Ighigeneia in Tauris', as narrated by the Greek dramatist Euripedes in the fifth century BC and made famous in more modern times in the works of a plethora of artists, musicians and writers, including Giovanni Battista Tiepolo, Wolfgang Amadaeus Mozart and Johann Wolfgang von Goethe. A most striking remnant of their culture today remains the Taurian stone dolmen (burial vault), constructed in the sixth–fifth centuries BC and situated on the slope of Mount Kishka near to what is today the coastal resort of Simeyiz, in the vicinity of Yalta.

During the middle of the third century BC, another nomadic equestrian people, the Sarmatians, intruded upon steppes north of Crimea, pushing the Sycthians to the east so as to establish their base in western Crimea. In reality, the Sarmatians were not one tribe but rather a loose federation including the Alans and the Roxolani. They too have come down to us today because of the reputation their female warriors acquired in battle, and have also been compared with the famous Amazons of Greek mythology and history.

By the second century BC, the independence of the Taurians had become curtailed by the powerful Scythian king Skilurus. Although the Scythians were by then waning in political terms, his reign from c. 124–113 BC was the final glorious flowering of the Scythian kingdom, before they too were forced to become a subject people. Numerous archaeological sites evincing their remains and relics have been explored over the last century throughout Crimea. Of these, the most imposing is the Tomb of Skilurus, near Simferopol, which shows the important influence of Hellenism in its construction and appearance. The Greek author Plutarch famously left an anecdote about Skilirus, in which the latter admonished his many offspring to choose unity over dissent with one another in order to maintain the success of the Scythian polity. Yet, in the long term, it would seem, his advice was not heeded, and it was left to a variety of new conquerors to establish their own temporary order on the peninsula.

By the end of the second century AD, it was the Alans, migrating from the lowlands along the eastern coast of the Sea of Azov and the Caucasus who made the most serious inroads into Crimea. Some established themselves along the coast at what is today Sudak, with its fortress, whilst others preferred the mountains where they founded settlements at what is now Chufut-Kale, as well as other such easily defended sites. There they took up agriculture and animal husbandry, whilst increasingly assimilating into the rest of the local population. In this sense, Crimea was and continues to be an extraordinary ethnic melting pot, which – in these days before the Mongol conquest – the adoption of Christianity eventually forged into a common identity which looked first towards Rome but later Byzantium, the 'Second Rome' and seat of the Byzantine Emperor or Emperor of the eastern half of the Roman Empire.

Goths

By the middle of the third century AD, as elsewhere throughout much of the Roman Empire, increasing political and social instability was erupting, to a large degree from pressure due to the ever more massive waves of nomadic immigration from beyond its frontiers. Of these, the Goths, who began their southward move from southern Sweden near the end of the second century AD, were among the most prominent. Unlike most invading tribes, which came from the north and east, the Goths arrived from the north and west. Those who migrated to the Black Sea littoral came to be known as the Ostrogoths or East Goths, distinct from their brethren, the Visigoths or West Goths who moved down over the Pyrenees into what was still Roman Spain, and North Africa.

By the middle of the third century AD, they had captured both the Scythian capital Neapolis (Simferopol), and the remains of the Bosporus Kingdom. They set their own mark on Crimea shortly thereafter, building the important fortress of Theodoro (Mangup), situated 14 kilometres east of Sevastopol, on the summit of a 475 metre high limestone plateau. In the fourth century AD, Bishop Ulfilas translated Biblical passages into western Visigothic – a language also understood by their eastern brethren – for the purposes of converting the Goths to Christianity.

It was about this time that the Ostrogothic Kingdom, ruled by its powerful King Ermanaric from 350–375 AD, reached its short-lived zenith. It encompassed not only all of Crimea but also parts of what is now mainland Ukraine. But, in 370 AD, before the end of his reign, he and the Gothic peoples, had to contend with the Huns. This fearsome equestrian people of Mongol ethnicity fell upon Crimea as they did upon much of Europe, raping, looting and pillaging whilst carrying off much of the surviving population into slavery. Those Ostrogoths who escaped this fate lay low in their mountain eyries, less accessible to the fleet footed cavalry of the Huns, more used to sweeping across the vast expanses and lowlands of the Eurasian steppes, and only cautiously reappeared after the deadly visitation had lifted, when the Huns retreated almost as suddenly as they had appeared. Whilst the Goths of Crimea disappeared as a political and ethnic entity, memories, indeed, a mythology of their presence during this long ago period remained latent. Yet a millennium later it would suddenly resurface in murderous form and to murderous effect: it became the ideological basis for the creation of a new Gothia, this one founded on Nazi ideology and, although it only lasted for a short period during the Second World War occupation by the Germans of Crimea, it led to the deaths of hundreds of thousands of Crimeans who did not even know that such a kingdom had ever existed.

Byzantine Crimea

That nightmarish Gothia was yet far in the future. Once again Byzantine hegemony – a polity in which the noble ideals of eastern Christianity were propagated, though by no means always put into action – reestablished itself in Crimea. Yet as the Roman Empire fell in the west, the Byzantine Empire persisted, indeed, often flourished, for over a millennium to come. In 381 the Arian heresy, proclaimed by Arius, a church presbyter from Alexandria, was condemned by the First Church Council of Constantinople because of its rejection of Trinitarian principles. Many Ostrogoths had come to adhere to this belief (along with some Byzantine emperors) but it was finally crushed in Crimea and Byzantine dogma and liturgy firmly accepted, not least through the efforts of its church's fifth-century bishop. He was appointed from Constantinople, now firmly in the Orthodox fold, and was based at Theodoro from where the Eparchy of Gothia was administered.

Byzantine links: political, cultural, spiritual and economic, deepened yet further under the rule of the renowned sixth-century Emperor Justinian I, who, in unifying his eastern empire, also established a unified Byzantine legal code, Justinian's Law for use throughout his domains and for which he is still justly famous. With Byzantine Crimea's capital established at Chersonesus, Justinian went on to create an elaborate system of defence for the peninsula, including the re-fortification of the Fortress of Theodoro, and the addition of other defensive fortifications to protect against further attacks emanating from the steppes to the north. These were carried out at present day Balaklava, Alushta, Hurzuf and Kerch. All these defensive implementations enabled Crimea to remain for centuries a bulwark of the Byzantine Empire. Later invasions and the destruction of the twentieth century have wiped out much of this heritage, but the Basilica of Constantine and Helen (ninth century), although later devastated, is still one of the best restored relics from this period, the devastation of an earthquake in the eleventh century, not withstanding. However, it was in the final centuries of Byzantine rule in Crimea, during the course of the later Middle Ages, that the region achieved its Golden Age of mercantile glory.

2

THE MIDDLE AGES

Byzantine Crimea and the Growing Power of Rus

During the early centuries of the Middle Ages, Crimea was predominantly Christian, under the influence first of the Byzantines and, later, of Kievan Rus. In south-western Crimea, the Byzantine Christian Goths, together with the Alans, reigned over Theodoro, from their mountain fortress at Mangup (14 kilometres west of today's Sevastopol) well into the eighth century. The kingdom was now a thriving and consolidated Greek-speaking Christian state. Indeed, much light was shed when the remnants of a lost sixth-century basilica, built by them at Chersonesus, was discovered by Soviet archaeologists in 1935. During the sixth and seventh centuries, new monasteries had been established by monks fleeing the iconoclastic upheavals and destruction which wrought havoc in Constantinople and elsewhere in the heartland of the Byzantine Empire. These were built in both the relatively remote mountainous interior and at coastal sites at what are today Inkerman and Bakhchisaray.

The power of Kievan Rus also increased from the tenth century and Kiev became the focus of Russian religious and political power to the north-west of Crimea, in particular, after its conversion to Byzantine Orthodoxy. As power was consolidated in the capital, so Kiev cast its glance east towards Crimea. Chronicles of the period confirm that the ruler of Rus, the Grand Prince Vladimir (r. 980–1015), was baptised in 988 in the ancient city of Chersonesos (on the south-west coast of Crimea near Sevastopol). This brought the multiplicity of peoples over which Kiev ruled into the Orthodox fold. The event would be commemorated in the late nineteenth century by one of the greatest Russian artists of that period, Viktor

Vasnetsov, in his Baptism of the Grand Prince St Vladimir (1890), a fresco in Kiev's St Vladimir's Cathedral.

Crimea's value for Kievan Rus was economic as well as religious – its salt, extracted from the north of the peninsula, was a major enticement. However, nomadic peoples from the east, in particular, the Tatar Kipchaks also laid claim to Crimea and its resources. These Tatars were in fact a vast conglomerate of Turkic-Mongol peoples who had arrived in the region both in advance and in the wake of the Mongol Hordes under Genghis Khan, and were eventually converted to Islam. Their leaders, nonetheless, formed marriage alliances of convenience with the princely Orthodox dynasty of Rus, and Crimea remained a multi-ethnic society, as long-settled peoples gradually made way for new more powerful settlers.

The Goths and the Khazars

The Goths, settled in Crimea since the late classical period, were amongst the first to suffer gradual displacement, in particular, by the arrival of the Khazars, another Turkic Tatar people from central Asia. They established themselves at Sudak and rapidly subdued both the northern steppes and the eastern coastal regions. Many of the previous inhabitants fled westwards to the coasts or into the mountains, where they survived in fortified strongholds. However, a revolt later in the century by the Gothic Prince and ecclesiastic Bishop John, based at the Mangup citadel, failed to throw off Khazar domination.

Even so, Byzantine Christianity continued to thrive, as did Byzantine church architecture. During the late ninth to early tenth centuries, the Church of St John the Baptist was built at Kerch and still functions today. Ironically, the Khazar khan had been supported by the Orthodox Christian Byzantine emperor. These Khazars had first come under the sway of Islam and then Judaism, they used Hebrew and followed many Old Testament traditions; Byzantine emperors, Justinian II and Constantine V, even married Khazar princesses. Moreover, the later arrival of the Byzantine forces from Constantinople established a period of relative stability which lasted until the turn of the next millennium. Then Byzantine power in the region waned. Nonetheless, the Gothic Princes of Theodoro maintained their presence for centuries, at the fourteenth century palace where they later established themselves when, during the first half of the fifteenth century, their power briefly revived. Under their powerful prince Aleksey, whose reign extended from 1405–55, they succeeded in subjecting much of the coast land again to their authority, an expression of their renewed interest in developing maritime trade. They turned Avilita into a major port, building the Fortress of Kalamita, today's Inkerman, to defend it. Cembalo (Balaklava) and Alushta also fell to them, at the cost of the Genoese, who had also gained a foothold in Crimea, thus ending the dichotomy which had for centuries separated the coast and its hinterland.

Armenians First Settle in Crimea

Meanwhile, during the mid eleventh century, the most ancient of Christian peoples, the Armenians, began to migrate into Crimea, following upheavals in their homeland of the southern Caucasus to the south-east of the Black Sea. Further waves of Armenians followed, as Armenia itself was subject to the increasing onslaughts of the Seljuk Turks. Kaffa (modern Feodosia) became the centre of Armenian life on the peninsula, but Solhat (Stary Krym), Karasubazar (Bilogorsk) and Orabazar (Armyansk) were also settled by them. There they thrived in both commerce and agriculture. These adherents of the Armenian Apostolic Church, said to have been established in Armenia as the world's first official Christian church in 301 AD, built their most important house of worship in Crimea, the St Sarkis (Sergey) Church, in Feodosia, in the fourteenth century; it functions as a place of worship to this day and is the burial place of the nineteenth-century Armenian maritime painter Ivan Aivazovsky.

Mongol Invasion and Subjection of Crimea

The most powerful people to invade Crimea during the Middle Ages were the Mongols. Indeed, this nomadic people were the greatest Eurasian conquerers of all time. The Mongol Hordes under Genghis Khan conquered Russia and reached into the European heartlands to the west, China to the east and the borders of Egypt to the south.

It was in 1222 that Mongol forces penetrated and conquered the lands which had been brought under the control of the Kipchaks. They reached as far as Crimea, devastating and pillaging Sudak and other rich mercantile port cities. The Kipchaks sought help from Kievan Rus, but even their joint forces proved to no avail. Crimea was subdued in 1338, by Batu Khan, grandson of Genghis Khan and founder of the Golden Horde, supported by some 120,000–140,000 men. Their superlative horsemanship had proved too overwhelming.[1] Indeed, the whole of Kievan Rus was brought under the 'Tatar yoke'.

Yet after the initial upheavals and massacres, Tatar domination proved not as onerous as later Russian and other Slavic nationalist mythology might imply. The surviving Kipchaks lost their common identity, instead merging with the new invaders. The surviving Christian inhabitants of Crimea soon carried on with their lives much as they had done under previous conquests. Indeed, the commercial networks of the Armenian merchants grew to encompass close relations with the Genoese who soon enjoyed a major presence in Crimea.

By the early fourteenth century there were two denominations of Armenian churches in Crimea: the Armenian Apostolic Church and the Catholic Armenian Church, which had come to accept Papal authority, with some forty-four churches throughout the region. They served what by now had become the second largest ethnic group residing in Crimea (the Tatars being the largest). As a result of this growing Armenian presence, the region became known in parts of western Christendom as *Armenia Maritima*, with a rich Christian culture famed for its high level of cultural development, not least because of its splendid tradition of manuscript illumination. Yet linguistic assimilation was occurring and many Armenians adopted the Tatar language, simply transliterating it into the Armenian alphabet. Indeed, this was a Golden Age for Crimea, one in which relative stability reigned, a symbiosis of all the peoples of the peninsula, whether Byzantine, Genoese or Tatar. Amongst the latter inhabitants of Crimea, Islam was a powerful presence, the evidence of which remains today. At Eski Krim, a short distance to the north of Sudak, the ruins of the Islamic seat of Özbeg, constructed by the order of the Mongol khan of the Golden Horde, still impress with the beauty and grace of its architecture.

Temporary Abatement of Tatar Hegemony

In 1380, at the Battle of Snipe Field by the River Don, the Tatars suffered a major defeat and the 'Tatar yoke' began to be lifted – albeit temporarily. Houses of worship were re-established, changing their religious focus according to the temporal powers who then held sway. In coastal Sudak, for example, St Matthew's Church was built on the site of a previous mosque. Constructed by Greek colonists as an Orthodox church, the Genoese reconsecrated it as a Catholic church after their arrival in the thirteenth century. With the arrival of Ottoman hegemony two centuries later, however, it reverted to use as a mosque and continued to function as such until 1783, the year Russia annexed Crimea, when, for the second time, it became an Orthodox church.

Although the Mongols conquered Crimea, the region suffered less of the appalling devastation at their hands than that afflicted on many of its subject peoples, the Great Khan largely contenting himself with the riches of Crimean tribute. Even the Principality of Theodoro ultimately survived. By the fourteenth century Mangup had become its capital, a vassal state of the Greek and Orthodox Gabras dynasty who ruled the Empire of Trebizond, to the south across the Black Sea in what is now north-eastern Turkey. It was at this time that a cadet branch immigrated to Moscow, where they became the hereditary treasurers of Muscovy, eventually assuming the name Golovin in the sixteenth century, just at the time the Muscovite tsars were beginning to turn their attention to Crimea.

Genoese

Another rival ethnic community to establish themselves in Crimea during the Middle Ages were the Genoese. The Republic of Genoa was a mercantile state which had acquired great riches and gone on to rival *La Serenissima* (the Venetian Republic), with which it vied for mastery of the extremely valuable trade with the East. Already in the 1280s, the Genoese had been encouraged by the Mongols, who had brought Crimea under their 'yoke', to establish warehouses at Kaffa for the goods with which they traded. From there it exported some 1,500 slaves every year, most providing manpower for the Mamluks of Egypt.[2] These slaves, owned by the sultan, formed a military cadre of great might, whose servile status belied the real power which they wielded. They were, moreover, not of Egyptian origin but were traditionally imported from the peoples of the Crimea and surrounding regions, famed for their stature and physical prowess. Other commodities which passed through the Genoese included grain and silk, the latter having made its way westward in caravans along the Silk Route from China. During the Middle Ages, this route led across the northern desert of China to Saray and thence across the steppes of Eurasia, north of the Caspian Sea to the Sea of Azov and on to the ports of Crimea. Many of the merchants who accompanied them stayed at the caravansary at today's Bilohirsk (Karasubazar), reconstructed from a former stone palace. Silks and other commodities were then shipped to other European ports, to Constantinople in particular, then the greatest emporium in the world.

However, the wealth and military might which made Kaffa a Genoese stronghold did not protect it from another onslaught – the arrival of the Black Death in 1347 – which went on to devastate virtually the entire western world. It is said that Khan Diani-Beg, besieging Kaffa that year, catapulted the heads of those of his own Tatar troops who had succumbed to the contagion, in order to infect the city. The exact form of transmission there remains unconfirmed but the outbreak of the plague in Kaffa is indisputable. Until it disappeared again in September 1348, no less than three quarters of the European settlers in Crimea and other Black Sea trading centres had perished.

The Genoese presence, nonetheless, survived and they were able to fortify themselves against successful attack by initiating the building of the great Fortress of Sudak, which successfully warded off attempts to subdue them until 1475. Indeed, by the time of its fall, nearby Kaffa had become one of the largest cities in Europe, with some 70,000 inhabitants. These were not only Genoese, but most importantly Armenians (who made up two thirds of the population), as well as a variety of Turkic speaking peoples, including Muslim Tatars, Jewish Krimchaks and Karaites. The latter had settled in Crimea in the mid thirteenth century; originating as a Jewish sect in Baghdad in the eighth century, and characterised by their rejection of the Talmud, they assimilated with other Turkic speaking peoples in Crimea, adopting a Tatar literary and vernacular language closely related to that of the Crimean Tatars. However, rather than using Arabic script, they used Hebrew for their liturgy and liturgical books. Besides Kaffa, they also settled at today's Stary Krym and then, in the wake of the final collapse of the Principality of Theodoro, at its former capital Mangup, as well as Chufut Kale.

There were also a great number of Byzantine Greeks, Wallachians originally from what is now Romania, and Slavs, originally from present day Russia and Ukraine. Nonetheless, it was the Genoese authorities, about a thousand in number, who administered this major trading emporium.

Crimea on the brink of the Ottoman conquest was highly multi-cultural. Armenians formed one of the largest communities, most of whom were members of the Armenian Apostolic Church. They were served by churches largely constructed in the fourteenth century in Yalta, Yevpatoria, Sudak and Feodosia (then Kaffa). In the latter alone, 46,000 out of a total of 70,000 inhabitants were said to be Armenian.[3] Of particular importance were the Gamchak Monastery, constructed in the fifteenth century and the Armenian community at Surkhat, which was spiritually centred around another monastery, that of Surb-Krach (Holy Cross). Finally there was Kazarat (near to Feodosia), the military stronghold of the Armenian princes which served the defensive needs of Feodosia. These were all served by an infrastructure of schools, banking houses and a caravanserai catering specifically for Armenians. A highly international ethnicity with trans-Mediterranean familial and trading links, many looked forward to reunion with the Catholic Church and were involved with relevant negotiations at the seventeenth Ecumenical Council which opened in Florence in January 1438, a difficult time for travel.

Establishment of Tatar Hegemony and Ottoman Annexation

During the early decades of the thirteenth century, the Seljuk Turks had firmly established themselves in Anatolia, to the south of Crimea, across the Black Sea. From this position of strength they extended their authority along a number of coastal areas, which soon included Sudak. However, their hegemony there had been short-lived. Nonetheless, during the second half that century, many Turks continued to arrive and settle on the peninsula, integrating with their fellow Muslims of the Golden Horde. At this stage, their presence did not necessarily imply conflict with the Genoese and Venetian merchants who were also setting there and benefiting all with their thriving trade. This was to a large degree because they made no attempt to undermine the authority of the Golden Horde, whose authority – military, political and spiritual – was based at Eski-Krim and who contented themselves with taking rich tributes, whilst taxing their mercantile activities.

A rich and powerful, dynasty, the Mausoleum of the Golden Horde princess Janike (early fifteenth century) evinces their Ghengisid status at this time, commemorating, as it does, this late lamented daughter of its fourteenth century ruler Tokhtamysh.

In 1428, Haci Giray, a contender to the khan's throne of the Golden Horde, left the steppes to seek refuge, and political and military support – not from fellow Muslim Turks but from the Catholic ruler of the Polish-Lithuanian Commonwealth. His ambitions were realised and he was finally invited by the Tatar clans to assume authority over them. He moved to Crimea in the late 1430s, as the first of the House of Giray, a Genghisid dynasty in its origins but one which declared its autonomy from the Golden Horde and which would reign over the Crimean Tatars until 1783, when Crimea itself was annexed by Russia. After Haci Giray's death in 1466, he was buried at Bakhchisaray, where he had established his beautiful Tatar capital. His successor Megli I Giray (1445–1515) was elected according to Tatar tradition.

The political and military context changed radically in 1475. Ottoman Turkish forces, under the authority of the sultan who, in 1453, had finally conquered Constantinople, now the seat of his empire and caliphate, captured not only Genoese Kaffa and their other port cities, but also their supposedly impregnable Theodoran Fortress of Mangup itself. All of Crimea was now subdued and became a vassal state of the Ottoman sultan. This conquest gave the Crimean khan Meghli I Giray valuable support from his immensely powerful Muslim neighbour across the Black Sea, which, together with that of the Grand Duke of Poland-Lithuania, to the north-west, enabled him to consolidate his dynasty and local authority – a de facto local autonomy. However, this was not true of the major ports, like Kaffa, which were placed directly under Ottoman military and administrative control. Turkish hegemony there by no means meant the economic decline of the ports. Indeed, Kaffa itself continued to thrive as one of Europe's most populous port cities and capital of this Ottoman provincial *sanjak* (province). Khan Meghli I Giray would have preferred to have had unfettered sovereignty over the whole of Crimea, but an annual pension from the sultan, together with rich land grants with lucrative revenues from elsewhere in the Ottoman Empire, in Anatolia and the Balkans, moderated his territorial ambitions.

Relations amongst the various khans of the steppes also brought practical benefits, in particular, Crimea's powerful Nogai Tatar allies, who lived to the north and east of the Caspian Sea. When the Khanate of Kazan ceased to maintain the good relations with Moscow it had formerly enjoyed, it came into the orbit of the other khanates. This enabled the Khanate of Crimea to see Kazan as a client state. In consequence, Kazan could be used as a stepping stone for reaching Moscow. In 1502, the Great Horde disappeared from amongst the great Tatar powers who held sway over the western steppes to the north of Crimea, superseded by the Khanate of Astrakhan. Moscow continued to stand in vassalage to the Tatar khans and, as late as 1504, some of the Tatar khans still received tribute from it. In the long term, however, this failed to protect Moscow from the growing southern and eastern threat. The Khanate of Crimea became increasingly stronger and, in 1521, the Crimean Tatars, aided by those of Kazan, now ruled by his brother Sahib I Giray, took the bold step of attacking Moscow itself. The city was vigorously defended by the Grand Prince Vasily III, with the assistance of his brother-in-law the tsarevich Peter Ibraimov. However, the Crimean Khan Mehmet Giray (1465–1523), who had ascended the throne in 1515, was reinforced by an ally to the west of Moscow, Zygmunt I the Old, king of Poland and Lithuania, with whom an alliance had been signed in 1520. The Grand Prince of Moscow was defeated near his capital by the jubilant Crimean Tatars.

3

THE CRIMEAN KHANATE AND OTTOMAN HEGEMONY

Establishment of the Khanate of Crimea

The Khanate of Crimea was first established in 1441 and survived for well over three centuries, until its annexation by Russia in 1783. For most of this period its capital was Bakhchisaray, where the palatial court of its khans was built – a smaller but very elegant version of the Topkapi Palace at Ottoman Constantinople under whose nominal sovereignty it remained for much of that period. Its ruler, a direct descendant of the first Mongol emperor Genghis Khan, ruled with a strong hand, his family protected by the irregular military forces known as the Sekbans who were local peasant soldiers at least 2,000 in number.

The original palace was a marvellous example of Islamic architecture and was built for the Crimean khan Mengli-Giray, by a Catholic architect known in Crimea as Aleviz, but christened Aloisio in his native Venice. He had first come to Crimea in the Venetian diplomatic entourage of Dimitry Ralev, the emissary sent from La Serenissima in 1500, and he eventually moved on to Moscow after the Bakhchisaray Palace was completed. There he designed and supervised the construction of one of Russia's most important houses of worship, the Cathedral of the Archangel Michael, in the Kremlin, the traditional burial site of the Russian tsars until the time of Peter the Great. That such an eminent architect should work in Crimea is not surprising, bearing in mind the incredible wealth which the Khanate accrued as a result of its maritime trade.

The Khanate of Crimea as an Ottoman Vassal State?

The Khanate of Crimea did not spring from the head of Zeus by its own independent efforts but rather established itself against the background of a growing regional Ottoman hegemony, which saw its own growing well-being reflected in that of its Crimean vassal but quite autonomous state. From their centuries-old territorial base in Anatolia these Ottoman Turks had succeeded in conquering not only the major cities of Anatolia but Constantinople itself, the capital and final bastion of the Byzantine Empire, in 1453. Then, rapidly, the Ottomans extended their authority across the Black Sea and into Crimea, obliging the then ruler of the dynastic house of Gabras to become their vassal. His sister, however, had married Prince Stephen III of Moldavia, and thus this prince felt sufficiently fortified by that relationship to lay claim to his brother-in-law's Theodoron throne. This he seized in early 1475. However, the Ottomans in the region, over whom the sultan's emissary Gedik Ahmet Pasha exerted authority, were not prepared to tolerate this change of rulers. In consequence, in May of that same year, they attacked the ancient Principality of Theodoro, conquering Kaffa and then laying siege to the Fortress of Mangup, which fell after a siege of five months. Thus, the centuries-old Christian Principality of Theodoro fell to the Ottomans. Mangup and Kaffa, with their environs, were now placed directly under the authority of the sultan in Constantinople, whilst authority over the rest of Crimea remained vested in the Crimean khan.

The exact nature of this Ottoman-Crimean relationship is a matter of continued contention. This new Ottoman vassal state was said to have been formally established by a treaty of 1478, signed by both Sultan Mehmet II (the Conquerer of Constantinople) and the Crimean khan Mengli Giray I. However, research from the 1940s as well as more recent analyses have led many to conclude that this was not the case. Rather, this research maintains that the Khanate of Crimea was an autonomous Tatar state throughout its existence, from 1478 until its annexation by Russia in 1783. If that is true then it would have been the only such Muslim state ever tolerated by the Turks in the European territories under their control throughout the many centuries of Ottoman hegemony. All others states under the nominal authority of the Sublime Porte were subsumed directly into the empire or permitted their national identity at a hefty price. Further recent historical research has created yet another scenario, one in which Crimea was an ally rather than a vassal state, even if, after 1584, the sultan, as the religious head of Islam, was prayed for before the khan at Friday prayers in the mosques of Crimea.[1] This was a circumstance which only changed during the mid seventeenth century, when Ottoman military, political and economic domination of Crimea became incontestable, its continued 'autonomous' status notwithstanding.[2]

Crimean Tatar Campaigns

One of the earliest military campaigns of the Crimean Tatars in the Ottoman period took place in 1476 when Crimean troops were sent to assist Sultan Mehmed II's forces in Moldavia, in the conquest of the ports of Akkerman and Kilia. This was not only intended to secure the north-western Black Sea littoral under Ottoman rule but to keep intrusions of the Polish-Lithuanian commonwealth at bay. It was Eminek Bey, leader of the Şirin clan in Crimea, who led the modest number of Tatar troops, but before they could be sent into action, Crimea itself was threatened by the Great Horde, a powerful Tatar people who, like the Crimean Tatars, had its origins in the earlier Golden Horde. However, in 1484, the Crimean Tatars returned to Moldavia and this time they did engage in battle, facilitating the successful conquest of Ackerman and Kilia by Ottoman sultan Bayed II, Mehmet II's successor.

In the first century of this Ottoman relationship, the Crimean khan only joined in military campaigns against Ottoman enemies when he perceived future benefits. Khan Sahib Giray wrote to the Sublime Porte:

> My sultan. The Tatar military is poor [literally; naked], has no means to go to a campaign so far away. But you can also not bring the Ottoman army [alone] to victory. ... I shall join the Ottoman army... If you do otherwise, you shall spend your money from your treasury in vain and will suffer many hardships.[3]

However, when Giray came to the view that a different military campaign would prove more beneficial to him, he jettisoned those of the sultan. Rather than fighting the Persians, therefore, he led his troops into battle against the Circassians, across the Straits of Kerch in the Caucasus. The Sublime Porte was not amused.[4] Over the following two centuries and beyond the Crimean Tatar Khanate was nonetheless an important military ally of the Ottomans in the Balkans, Ukraine, the Caucasus and the western frontier lands of Persia, and this the Sublime Porte realised.

It was the Poland-Lithuanian Commonwealth during the sixteenth century which was seen as both the greatest threat to Ottoman expansion, and as its greatest source of slaves and booty, mostly through Crimean Tatar intermediaries. So, in 1524, the government of the commonwealth invited the Zaporozhian Cossacks – a group of largely Slavic Orthodox peoples who lived in the Tatar borderlands of what is today central Ukraine – to permanently settle near the borders of the Ottoman Empire and Khanate of Crimea, to render the Poles and Lithuanians assistance as a frontier force. From now on, first fitfully but then, in the later seventeenth century, unrelentingly, Cossack incursions into Crimea brought the raiding, by which the Crimeans lived, rebounding into their own backyard and eventually onto what had become a veritable Ottoman lake, the Black Sea, thereby disrupting the trade not only of goods but of slaves.[5]

Tatar military campaigns were frequently of long duration. Indeed, with respect to Hungary, they went on for centuries: Crimean Tatars played a major role in the conquest of Hungary by the Ottomans as early as 1521 and were still active in that of Transylvania in 1718; they were even to be found at the apogee of Ottoman power, in the heartland of Europe, when Vienna itself was besieged in 1683.[6]

This was also the case in the Middle East, for the Crimean Tatar contribution to the virtually endless Ottoman battles with Persia under the Safavid dynasty, was of considerable importance. With their aid, Ottoman sultan Selim I defeated the Persians at Chaldiran and Tabriz in 1514, conquests which led to Ottoman hegemony in these regions under his son, Sultan Süleyman the Magnificent.

Thus, during the seventeenth century, the Crimean Tatars were continuously drawn into battle with their Ottoman allies in both the east and the west. Not all were successful: the siege at Khotyn, in Moldavia, in 1621, was unsuccessful, failing to overwhelm the resisting military forces of the Polish-Lithuanian Commonwealth. By contrast, that of Kamieniec, in Podolia (today's south-western Ukraine), effected by some 80,000 troops, including those from Crimea, proved a major, if short lasting, victory: the Treaty of Buczacz ceded Podolia to the Sublime Porte. In 1700, however, Russia, under its great warrior tsar Peter the Great, nullified this cession by the Treaty of Constantinople, thereby increasing Russian authority over the Cossacks who were based there. The result was that both the Ottomans and the Crimean Tatars, now increasingly subordinated to the Sublime Porte, were on the back foot. This weakness led to the increasing subordination of Crimea to the Ottomans. The khans, instead of following the tradition of succeeding according to Tatar tradition, were increasingly chosen by the Ottomans from the ruling Giray dynasty. This was done, not according to the Christian European tradition of the eldest son, nor even necessarily by the Turkic tradition of the eldest male relation, but rather according to who might most benefit the Sublime Porte. This was obviously the case in 1702, when Devlet II Giray was obliged by the Sublime Porte to relinquish his throne to its own chosen candidate from the House of Giray, despite his popularity amongst the other Crimean leaders.[7] This weakness, however, did not mean that the end of the Khanate was imminent, that direct annexation would follow. On the contrary, the Ottomans were strengthening their position vis-à-vis Russia through the maintenance of an independent, though debilitated, Crimea, one which it was hoped would be able to arrest the advance of Russian armies under the tsar, as occurred at the Prut River in 1711. Whatever its benefits to the Ottomans, though, it terminally undermined the integrity of Crimea. This was the conclusion of a process which Russia had taken decades to achieve by constantly forcing the Ottomans and Crimea to curb their intrusions with costly campaigns. None of this, of course, undermined the strength of Crimean Tatar identity. For the trident-shaped heraldic symbol of the Giray dynasty (tamga) was then and remains even now — an important symbol of their former strength. Then, it was displayed not only by the portals of the council chamber of the Crimean khans, but also on the coinage and the diplomatic treaties which it signed. Even today it symbolises the past and present glories of the Tatars — regardless of modern Ukrainian and now Russian sovereignty over Crimea. [8]

First Capital of the Crimean Tatars

The first capital of the Crimean Khanate was established at today's Stary Krym (in Tatar both Sokhat and Krim). However, Khan Haji Giray (r. 1441–66) transferred it to the fortress-like town of Kirk Yer (Chufut-Kale, a Tatar term signifying a Jewish Fortress, since many Jews had previously settled in that region), in the mountains near Bakhchisaray. He himself preferred to reside, however, in luxurious surroundings in the valley below, at today's Starosillia (in Tatar: Salachik). This khan's village, in fact, became quite a centre of Islamic culture and theology, especially after 1500, the year in which his son and successor Mengli I Giray added a Muslim seminary for the education of Crimean mullahs, to what had become an extensive palace. The impressive mausoleum of these early khans, built in 1501, is still there in much of its glory. Eventually, though, this site became too constrained and the latter's son Khan Sahib I Giray (r. 1532–50) re-established the capital, along with the construction of a new palace complex, at Bakhchisaray already in the first year of his reign. Kirk Yer then reverted to its former identity as a centre of Jewish life, in particular, for the Turkic Karaites.

As for Mangup and Theodoro, the ancient sites of the originally Byzantine principality, neither ever recovered from the subjection of Crimea to the Tatars and Ottomans. This final breath of the classical age of Greece and Rome had been extinguished. Yet the architectural remains of their former glory continued to astonish rare Christian visitors even at the height of Crimean Tatar hegemony. One such visitor to appreciate them was the Polish aristocratic emissary Marcin Broniewski, who arrived on a mission to the Crimean khan Mehmet Giray, in 1579. His Latin commentary on the visit appeared a century later in an English version entitled *Marcopia*, translated by Samuel Purchas. It noted that Mangup then 'hath two Castles, Greeke Temples and Houses sumptuous, with many cleer Rils running out of the stone: but eighteen years after the Turkes had taken it (as the Christians affirm) it was destroyed by a sudden and horrible fire.'[9]

The Karaites were the last of the peoples to settle around Mangup. They were a Turkic people descended from the Khazars, who had adopted a highly Judaised version of Islam which set them radically apart from their other Tatar neighbours. They were also the last to depart, about the time of the annexation of Crimea to Russia in 1783, as the remains of their cemetery of that time confirm.

Persecution of Christians with the Arrival of Ottoman Hegemony

A plethora of ethnic communities, of diverse religious beliefs, resided in the Khanate throughout this period, much as elsewhere in the Ottoman

Empire. Christians included the Alans, Greek Orthodox Christians, and the Sarmatian pastoralists who had previously been settled in the North Caucasus. The Sarmatians dwindled in number under Muslim rule, but they remained physically distinctive because of their tradition, adopted from the Huns, of binding the heads of their children, to give them an egg-shaped form.[10]

Yet despite the reputation for religious tolerance said to have been enjoyed by Christians under Ottoman authority, the Christian population of Crimea, during and after the Ottoman conquest and consolidation of their hegemony, suffered an unequivocal catastrophe. Sixteen Armenian churches were confiscated and turned into mosques, whilst the Armenian population, in particular, suffered serious depredations. Massacres occurred and many were sold into slavery. Those more fortunate fled abroad, became useful to the Tatars or endeavoured to weather the upheavals in mountainous areas as best they could. Nevertheless, sizeable numbers of Armenians continued to populate Crimea, despite the decimations of the post-Ottoman conquest. During the sixteenth century, the Armenians even enjoyed a modest revival, not only in and around Kaffa and the towns which had long been home to Armenians, but also in Balaklava, Gezlev and Perekop. Their commercial networks reached throughout the Mediterranean and brought benefits to the Tatars, as well as the Ottomans so that a minority of mercantile Armenians thrived in consequence.

Crimean Sack of Moscow and Russian Expansion Southward

It was Russia, in the first two centuries of the Crimean Tatar Khanate which particularly suffered from the depredations of the Tatars. In 1521, Crimean khan Mohammed Giray launched a devastating attack on Moscow which laid waste to much of the city. They were then thrust back. However, when in 1552, the Russian Tsar Ivan the Terrible conquered Kazan, then under the sovereignty of a member of the Crimean Tatar Giray dynasty, the Crimean Tatars determined to reassert their authority. The khan found a formidable ally in the Ottoman sultan and together, in 1569, they attacked Astrakhan to the north-east, which had fallen to the Muscovites, keen to control the Volga for trade, as well as access to the lucrative markets of Persia to the south-west. The symbolism of this loss to their Ghengisid heritage was a potent threat to Crimean Tatar authority in the region, especially vis-à-vis the Ottomans. Although this campaign failed to retake Astrakhan, it did succeed in wreaking havoc in Moscow, which was raided by the Crimean Tatars and their allies again in 1571. This occurred only one year after the tsar had devastated the rich, independent Russian cities of Novgorod and Pskov, which had, in turn, threatened his imperialistic designs, and laid waste to vast tracts of the agriculturally productive countryside over which they had formerly ruled. He could then turn his attention to the Tatars and in 1572, Ivan's forces successfully secured Moscow, if not the provinces, against their depredations.

The Crimean Tatar Cavalry

Nonetheless, the Crimean Tatar cavalry – approximately 10,000 strong in peacetime but double that when the khan led his men into battle – was a force to be reckoned with throughout the sixteenth century. By the latter half, it was principally composed of the khan's own men, led by members of the ruling family. These, in turn, were augmented by those of other great families of the Khanate as well as those of the other important Tatar ethnos to the north of Crimea, the Nogai Tatars. In 1547, Baba Bey, leader of the Şirin clan, assisted his overlord, Crimean Tatar khan Sahib Giray, with 5,000 of his own men who marched with their own military band; the Bann, Argın and Kipçak clans also provided men. The Sublime Porte also made sure that Ottoman infantry units, generally Janissaries (originally Christian boys from Ottoman Balkan territories taken from their families in levy to act later as highly trained shock troops after forced conversion to Islam) played a major role. The Ottomans contributed a similar 5,000 men, along with 300 Janissaries, the cost of which was borne by them. The khan of Crimea made use of modern weaponry, employing Tatar and Circassian musketeers, some 500 in number, by the end of the sixteenth century.[11] Some historians have estimated Tatar strength even higher, as much as 30–40,000 men strong in the sixteenth century, and 40–60,000 strong in the seventeenth century. That said, many of these would have been stationed in Crimea itself, with only a fraction of that number actually sent elsewhere into battle.[12] In this period the disruptive power of the united Crimean forces was considerable and they carried off tens of thousands of Christian slaves, from Muscovy, the Polish-Lithuanian Commonwealth and the Caucasus.

The role of the Crimean Tatars in Ottoman campaigns grew in significance over time. Indeed, as the Ottomans set their eyes on hegemony over Hungary, the khan and his Tatars played a crucial role; in 1596 alone, the Sublime Porte sought the aid of up to 80,000 men to assist them in its conquest. The Sublime Porte made its 'request' for troops by means of imperial letters, delivered in highly symbolic fashion with inlaid swords and richly embroidered kaftans as accompanying 'gifts.' These were sent in such a way as to show respect for the khan as a Gengisid descendant of the original Mongol emperor and founder of his dynasty and therefore an equal of the Ottoman sultan himself – in terms of status at least, if not of military might. Whereas usually, during the winter months, such forces returned to their homeland, during the Hungarian adventure, this was not the case. In 1603, the Crimean khan himself continued to reside in Hungary with up to 40,000 of his men.[13]

However, as the seventeenth century wore on, the respect shown by the Sublime Porte to the Crimean khan diminished. With Sultan Süleyman the Magnificent's growing renown and glory, the disparity of power between the Ottomans and the Crimean Tatars had grown too great for such mutual respect: henceforth, the Ottoman Grand Vizier, from the time of Sinan Pasha, began to treat the Crimean khans as inferiors, their Gengisid ancestry notwithstanding.[14]

The Balkans and the Crimean Tatars

The movements of the Crimean Tatar cavalry and ancillary forces did not bode well for the people, especially in the Balkans, across whose land they travelled, whether friend or foe. Dobruja, on the western shores of the Black Sea, Wallachia (now southern Romania), and present-day Serbia, lying along the Danube River, were frequently ravaged, even when under the sovereignty of the sultan. The khan Gazi Giray himself noted in 1600, in a letter to the Sublime Porte:

> If I went to Dobruja, the province would not recover for ten years afterwards. Wallachia and Transylvania would also be laid ruin, and would be uninhabitable for years. Hurry back with the permission, which route would be the right one.[15]

In this instance Dobruja was chosen. It had a large Turkish population but elsewhere in Christian Wallachia and Serbia, it was the Orthodox Christian subjects of the sultan who were obliged to provide the food and forage for the troops required. These were not provided so much on the spot during the passage but beforehand to the Crimean ports of Gözleve (10,000 kilos each of wheat, barley, and flour in advance of the 1578 campaign) and Kaffa (10,000 kilos of flour, barley, and millet). Not surprisingly, the Prince of Transylvania, a Christian vassal of the Ottomans, did all in his power to convince the Sublime Porte of the need to choose a route away from his principality. Yet even the sultan himself sometimes had difficulties in getting the Crimean Tatars to follow his commands, even with respect to the route to be taken by them across his own territory.[16] Sometimes an out-and-out bribe was required, as in 1621, when Transylvanian Prince Gábor Bethlen (1613–1629) tempted the Tatar envoy with 1,000 gold coins. This offer, however, proved in vain, since the ultimate decision rested with the highest military command of the Sublime Porte itself. Either way, the Crimean khan, accompanied by the Aga sultan, his heir and second in command, coveted the far greater rewards which a successful campaign could bring.[17] Indeed, it was Kalga Şahin Giray, who led the Tatar auxiliary troops, who assisted Gábor Bethlen in wars against the Austrian Habsburgs and in his successful ascent to the Transylvanian throne, when the latter provided him with the future reward of no less than the value of 5,000 gold coins. 1,000 of them were provided in the equivalent of gunpowder, 2,000 in fine cloth and the rest money. However, the opposite happened in 1657, when the sultan commanded the Tatars to obstruct Prince György Rákóczi II of Transylvania's military campaign against Poland, thereby restricting the extension of their territorial expansion at the latter's expense. Clearly, the Crimean Tatars' were a force to be reckoned with in central Europe, as far back as 1598, whose interference served to arbitrate both victory and defeat for allies and foes alike. For this reason the Habsburgs maintained close diplomatic relations with the Tatars whose exotically attired envoys became a seasonal sight in Vienna from 1662. Even before that time though, since the beginning of the Long Turkish War (1593–1606), the Tatars were in contact with Vienna. This ultimately led to the Treaty of Zsitvatorok, which ended the long war between Austria and the Ottoman Empire. Moreover, the Tatar network of foreign envoys was not limited to the

Habsburgs. It extended to Scandinavia (Sweden from 1591, Denmark from about 1650), Russia, the German states (Brandenburg from about 1650) and Persia. They were also useful negotiators when arbitration was required between the Ottomans and their Christian subjects. Thus, in 1595, Crimean khan Gazi Giray II served in this role at the Peace of Tutora, in Poland, and in 1676, Khan Selim Giray was Ottoman emissary at Žuravno, when peace was made in Poland.[18]

Sometimes, the Crimean Tatars turned the tables on the Ottomans at which point the Christians became their allies against the Turks. In 1599, for example, Khan Gazi Giray II formed an alliance with Prince Zsigmond Báthory of Transylvania, against an official backdrop of his role as a go-between for the Ottomans and the Hapsburgs. Though such an alliance was short-lived, as the interests of the individual parties changed, one such example was when, during the First Great Northern War, the Tatars allied with Poland against Transylvania, who were at this time allies of the Swedes. The quest for territorial aggrandisement was important, but equally, the role of economics should not be underestimated: Crimea, as a major mercantile hub, wanted to remove the customs burdens imposed by those with whom it traded as much as possible and this aspect played a role in the treaties agreed, especially with the Christian countries to the west.[19]

Tatar Slave Raids

Slave raids were a principal source of income for the Crimean Tatars and played a key role in their wars. Tatar envoys were also important go-betweens for more than 250 years when ransoms were demanded for important Christians captured in raiding. After the Ottoman-Tatar subjection of Crimea, the slave trade from Crimea to the Mediterranean world and Middle East increased dramatically, especially during the course of the sixteenth century. It was *haram* (forbidden) to enslave faithful Muslims according to Sharia law, but Christians were fair game. In consequence, Tatar raids northwards from Crimea grew more and more daring, providing the Ottoman Empire with its principal source of slaves. At the same time, the blindness of the Tatars, on various occasions, as to who was and who was not a Muslim, meant that those enslaved were not always Christian prisoners, nor were the owners of goods taken as booty.

This circumstance was a constant source of friction with the Ottomans who took umbrage at the exploitation of fellow Muslims, especially so when the Crimeans Tatars, at almost constant war in the 1570s–80s, saw them as legitimate targets for slave raiding and booty, to the great consternation of the Ottomans and their spiritual advisers. [20]

Yet it was Muscovy and the neighbouring Poland-Lithuanian Commonwealth which bore the brunt of these raids. No less than eighty onslaughts had been made on both in this period, with the participation of up to 30,000 troops. In 1575, more than 35,000 Christians were carried off to be sold in the markets of Kaffa and other Crimean ports. The most famous such captive was the sultana Roxelana (born Alexandra Lisowska but known as Hürrem Sultan, in Turkish; 1506–58). Carried off as a slave from Poland, she was first sent to Kaffa and thence to Constantinople, where her beauty and charm led to her acquisition by the Ottoman sultan Suleyman the Magnificent himself. Converted to Islam, she entered the sultan's harem, in which she achieved the highest status possible for a woman in the Ottoman Empire, first as premier consort and then as official wife. But as the Englishman Richard Knolles wrote in *The Generall Historie of the Turkes*, published in 1603:

To fairest lookes trust not too farre, nor yet to beauty braue:
For hateful thoughts so finely maskt, their deadly poisons haue.
Loues charmed cups, the subtile dame doth to her husband fill:
And causeth him with cruell hand, his childrens bloud to spill. [21]

As Valide Sultan (Mother of the sultan), she was the power behind the throne of her son Sultan Selim II, who succeeded Suleyman the Magnificent, but even during Suleyman's lifetime she connived to remove one of her harem rivals and successfully encouraged the sultan to have Mustafa, her rival's son by the sultan, put to death.

Of course, the life of the sultana Roxelana was quite extraordinary for a former Christian captive; for the overwhelming majority of slaves, such lofty prospects were out of the question. Generally even prized Christian captives, whose kidnappings were expected to bring in considerable ransoms, fared poorly, imprisoned, sometimes for years, in Crimean fortresses. On the other hand, favoured ones might even benefit from the captivity by forming useful relationships which might have political uses after their release to their home country. This was the case with János

Kemény and Mihály Apafi, princes of Transylvania, who were kept captive in Crimea, the latter in the fortress of Or. He remained in contact with his captor Karaş Bey, even after he assumed the throne of Transylvania. Such an arrangement was, of course, useful to the Crimean khan, but the primary motivation of the slave trade for the Crimean Tatars was money. For the khan not only benefited from the sale of his own slaves but from tolls charged on the trade itself in his domains.[22]

Slave raiding did not, however, always prove successful. In 1572, Khan Devlet I Giray (1512–77) and his hordes, said to number over 120,000 men, were decisively defeated at the Battle of Molodi, just south of Moscow, by forces of half that number, led by the highly able Prince Mikhail Vorotynsky. The khan not only lost 100,000 of his soldiers but his sons and a grandchild as well. This allowed a respite in the south, enabling the tsar to turn his aggressive attentions westwards towards the Baltic region. By restraining the Crimean Tatars, Russia was able to pursue its long term goal of extending its territorial hegemony deeper into the eastern reaches of the central European states. Internally, there were also repercussions, because the obvious failure of Ivan the Terrible's feared *Oprichnina* (shock troops or secret police) led to their disbanding that same year. Of course, Slavs were not the only victims of slave raiding. Karbardinian slaves from the Caucasus to the east also brought in high premiums in Ottoman Constantinople, although the Crimean Tatars had to compete with their slave raiding rivals the Kalmyks, who raided the Karbadinians from further east. Kaffa, was the Crimean focal point of this human cargo, situated on the southeastern coast of Crimea with excellent maritime connections all around the Black Sea littoral. This situation, however, led the Karabadian Prince Temriuk Idarov and his supporters to forge an alliance with Ivan the Terrible. Indeed, he married off one of his daughters to the widower Ivan, after the death of his first wife. She converted to Orthodoxy, taking the name Maria. Nonetheless, the slave trade continued and became ever more essential for not only the domestic needs of the Ottomans, but their naval defence as well: the galley slaves which the Crimean Tatars provided the Sublime Porte were necessary for its very survival.[23]

Slaves were, of course, not the only important commodity traded through Crimea. Wine had for centuries been a mainstay of the economy but this ceased dramatically with the arrival of the Muslim Tatars, because of its the prohibition under Sharia Law. By the 1590, the strengthening of Muscovite authority southwards and eastwards into Tatar territory led to the weakening of the Nogai Khanate and their eventual submission to Muscovite rule. In consequence, the buffer zone between the Grand Principality and the domains of the Crimean Khanate diminished, replaced by a long frontier which on Russian side was now defended by numerous fortified towns such as Voronezh, Kursk and Belgorod. Not only now were the Crimeans beleaguered by the Russians, but they also had to contend with the enemies of their Ottoman allies, including the Poles, Lithuanians and Austrians in the west, and the Persians to the southeast. Long past were the days when the Crimean Tatars could boast of being the full heirs of the Golden Horde, for, unlike the latter, they did not have a cavalry of significant firepower. The Ottomans, moreover had no desire to make the Crimean Tatars so powerful that they might one day turn against them. This was no paranoid fear: khans Mehmed Giray II (1584) and Mehmed Giray III (1624) both tried to wrest Kaffa away from the Ottomans by laying siege to this great Crimean city, but to no avail. The Crimean Tatars lagged ever more behind with respect to keeping pace with the latest innovations in military technology, to which not only their western enemies but sometimes even their Ottoman allies were party.[24]

Continued Forays into Russia

The Crimean Tatars did not wage conventional military warfare or lay siege to cities as such for, as Khan Gazi Giray II put it in a letter to the high Ottoman official, Sa'adeddin Hoca, who had been tutor to Sultan Murad III: 'Besieging castles is not the task of Tatars; it is rather to ravage, desolate, and ransack the infidels' country with their raids, and also to collect captives and provisions.'[25] Yet for all his religious fervour in focusing his raids upon 'the infidels' country', he had few qualms in offering to assist 'infidel' Poland against their common 'infidel' enemy Russia, at least if they promised him five thousand gold coins in exchange.[26] Nonetheless, these Tatar raids tended to be characterised by features peculiar to Islam and Sharia law. Within Crimea itself, it was the *kadis*, the judicial authorities, who administered strict justice and laid down rulings for Muslims. Non-Muslims, however, were open game. Christian villages were attacked as a matter of course with both humans and animals carried off. Of domestic animals only pigs were rejected, because of their Qur'anic uncleanliness and they were gathered together in stables to be burnt alive. Christians who were felled were abandoned where they lay, but the Tatar warriors themselves rarely left their bodies to the enemy. Instead, they gathered them up, to be incinerated on great funeral pyres. Morale was high and their ethnic and religious identity helped fuse together a common military and economic purpose. This meant that the Crimean Tatars were always a force to be reckoned with. Their cavalry were immensely skilled with the bow and arrow, which could hit targets farther away than the guns of their enemies. Moreover, the guns took longer to reload than the bows. This enabled the Tatars to apply the same techniques against their human prey, as against the game which they long had pursued on the steppes as a nomadic people: showering them with arrows in ever smaller concentric circles.[27]

In 1591, the Crimean khan Gazi Giray made particularly devastating inroads deep into Russia, once again threatening Moscow on the outskirts between the Kaluga and Tula roads. This time, however, Muscovite forces, under Tsar Boris Gudonov kept him at bay, using a transportable wooden fortress first developed under Ivan the Terrible. The Crimean khans' major weaknesses had been revealed by the modern European technology successfully deployed against them, so this was the last attempt they made to attack the suburbs of Moscow.

With the dawn of the seventeenth century, the fierce and growing strength of the Don Cossacks (the latter term signifies 'free people', unencumbered by feudal obligations and usually of Slavic ethnicity) increasingly came to be used by Moscow to repel attackers and to extend Russian hegemony to the south. Their growing settlement on the River Don, in what came to be known as Ukraine (the name signifies a border region) and their warlike disposition made them excellent shock troops against the weakening Muslim khanates. These included the Tatar vassal states of the Khan of Crimea, the Yedisan, Yedichkul and Dzhambulak hordes.

Nonetheless, in 1642, after an extended lapse, Tsar Mikhail Romanov, founder of the dynasty which would rule Russia until 1917, reluctantly renewed his consent to pay tribute to the Khan of Crimea to ward off renewed Tatar forays at a time when Muscovy was only just recovering from a lengthy period of troubles. Such a tribute as this, both from Russia as well as from the Polish-Lithuanian Commonwealth, was still significant. Indeed, it formed a major part of the khan's income.[28] This occurred despite the exhortations of Mikhail Romanov's advisers to refuse. However, the tsar was all too aware that the Khanate of Azov, recently conquered in the east after a long siege, by the Don and Zaporozhian Cossacks, could not be held. Famines and epidemics, moreover, were raging throughout the region.

Crimea itself had its own problems to contend with, since internal factions were warring with one another. Then, in 1644, Islam Giray III (1644–54) ascended the Crimean throne, and Muscovy once again came under threat. With the assistance of some 40,000 Tatar soldiers under Tughay-Bey, commander of the Or-Kapi fortress at Perekop, the internal anarchy was quelled and he succeeded in wreaking havoc amongst both the Don and Zaporozhian Cossacks. Moscow itself was attacked from the south, although the city once again held off against the intruders, but the old tsar was weak and failing, dying shortly thereafter. His son Aleksey succeeded to the throne in 1646 and made his first goal the bolstering of the southern borderlands against future assaults by the Crimean Tatars and their Ottoman allies. To do this, he established the Belgorod Line, a string of garrison towns settled and defended by the Cossacks against Tatar attack.

With respect to the commonwealth, however, the situation was more confused. The Polish Lithuanian rulers could not always rely on the Cossacks to defend them. This was a grave matter as throughout the sixteenth century until 1664, over a million people had been carried off as slaves.[29] Nor could the Cossacks always be relied on. In 1648, Bohdan Khmelnytsky (c.1595–1657), the hetman of the Zaporozhian Cossacks, formed an alliance with the Crimean Tatars, under Khan Islam Giray III (r. 1644–54). Together they imposed two stunning defeats on the forces of the commonwealth, followed by a third in 1652. Ukraine was being torn asunder, as Poles, Lithuanians, rebel Cossacks and Muscovites vied for control of as much of the region as they could seize and defend from further attacks. This led Moscow to impose its authority ever more heavily on the Don Cossacks, not so much through military means but through a range of financial subsidies. Consequently, in 1654 Hetman Khmelnytsky swore cossack loyalty to Moscow, under a treaty signed at the city of Pereiaslav in central Ukraine (in 1943 it was renamed Pereiaslav-Khmelnytsky in his honour by the returning Soviet army).

Maritime measures were also taken against the Crimean Tatars. Moscow initiated naval activity on the Don some of which was directed against the Ottomans, who were building new fortresses in the region, though at other times, this activity was directed against the Cossacks themselves. It was the Tatars, however, who benefited most from this factionalism amongst their foes. If the Cossacks could ally themselves with the Tatars, what benefit were they to the tsar? This hit home in particular when Hetman Petro Doroshenko came to the aid of the Ottomans in 1672, against the Commonwealth. But factionalism existed amongst the Cossacks as well and an alliance with the 'infidel' Turks did not sit well with many of his devoted Orthodox cohorts. In 1676 he was forced to abdicate and moved into exile in Moscow; Ivan Samoylovich then became hetman. Supported by Moscow, he followed a Moscow-inspired political and military line.

The relationship of the Crimean khans to all their neighbours was, thus, quite complex and full of shifting alliances. It was, therefore, incumbent upon them, to keep a heightened awareness of the slightest changes that took place, in order to best deal with them. To do so, they established an intricate network of spies as early as the mid-seventeenth century. These were by no means restricted to the Tatars themselves, or even their Ottoman allies, but Christian Europeans as well, who had command of the various European languages of central and eastern Europe, as far afield as the German heartland. In consequence, the Crimean intelligence network was by no means unsophisticated.

Cultural Richness of Crimea

For all its dependence upon slave raiding, Crimea was hardly a barbaric state devoid of intellectual and cultural ferment. On the contrary, its khans, no less than the Ottoman sultans, were highly educated and culturally refined. They were also very literate – after all Islam is a 'religion of the book' – and the palace at Bakhchisaray boasted a splendid library, until the Russians burnt it down during the siege of the town in 1736. It was the sojourn of Khan Gazi Giray II in Hungary during the later sixteenth century which brought an awareness of his literary activities to the wider European world. He wrote poetry – still read today – and impressed the Hungarian chronicler, István Szamosközi, who observed that a camel-load of books accompanied him on every campaign. He was also known to be musical, a gifted composer and accomplished player of various musical instruments, performing the music of his time as well as his own works, still performed today as a part of the classical Turkic repertoire.[30]

Crimea was also a land possessed of a great internal linguistic richness and variety. Hebrew, Greek and Gothic were three of the ancient languages still spoken in Crimea at this time. Indeed, in 1562, the Austrian diplomat Ogier Ghislain de Busbecq – who introduced the tulip bulb to western Europe from the Ottoman Empire – listed some eighty-six Gothic words, along with numerous Gothic phrases, provided by native Crimeans he encountered in Constantinople. His writings have led some scholars to maintain that Gothic only became a dead language in the end of the seventeenth century, even though many scholars set the date much earlier.

Russian Military Campaigns against Crimea

When in the 1670s, the Crimean Tatars were further weakened, despite Ottoman support, the Donskoy Monastery in Moscow, first associated with Boris Gudonov and his success against Khan Gazi Giray, became the centre of commemorative liturgies related to their containment. In this regard, Prince Vasily Golitsyn played a significant role because of his encouragement of Moscow's aggressive approach to reducing the Crimean Tatars. As a result of this, he undertook two major campaigns against them in 1687 and 1689. Largely unsuccessful, these had the deleterious effect of undermining the regency of Tsaritsa Sophia (1682–89) during the minority of Peter the Great. However, upon his ascension to the throne, he renewed support for Russia's expansion to the south, at the cost of the Tatars, Crimea and Nogai, albeit in a less confrontational manner, with respect to Crimea itself.

The first of the Tatar dominoes began to fall when Peter captured the mouth of the River Don, at the Battle of Azov, in 1696. This was the beginning of the end of Tatar hegemony in the region. Slave raiding dwindled to a trickle and soon ceased altogether during Peter the Great's reign. It also opened Russia up to Europe and the Mediterranean world to the south, for in the long perspective, Crimea was Russia's principal, albeit, far southern bridge.

To accomplish this the Russians made use of some non-Russian ethnic peoples, who had subjected themselves to the Russian tsar. Among the most important of these were the Mongol Kalmyks, a nomadic people who had recently arrived in the area to the north and east of the Sea of Azov. Their importance is reflected in the fact that they were adherents to Buddhism, which is today one of Russia's four religions granted a special historical status (with Orthodoxy, Islam and Judaism). Through a treaty of 1655, the Kalmyks committed themselves to loyally serve the tsar, carrying out their own raids into Crimea, at the expense of both Tatar and Ottoman interests, both of which they gradually undermined.[31] So successful were their attacks and those of several other neighbouring peoples of the Crimean Tatars that, after 1700, Peter the Great ceased all payments of tribute to the Crimean khans.

To stem this Russian tide, the Ottomans built the Fortress of Yenikale, near Kerch, between 1699–1706. Yet this only temporarily halted, rather than stopped, the Russian inroads. At first it seemed as if the Zaprozhian Cossacks, who had so energetically served the interests of Russia in the late seventeenth century, would now tip the balance in favour of the Crimean Tatars and their Ottoman allies. For in 1709, they had assisted the Swedes, under their warrior king Karl XII, in their battle against Peter the Great and the Russians. However, with the failure of the Swedes and the success of the tsar, they had found themselves on the losing side. In punishment, the tsar abolished the Sich, their home settlement to the north of Crimea, and forbade them from entering Russian territory with arms. In consequence, the very people who had for almost two centuries defended the frontiers of Christendom went over to the Crimean Tatars. The latter seemed to have won a reprieve from Russian depredations. However, this unnatural arrangement proved short-lived. In 1733, the Cossacks returned to the Russian fold through a pardon of Peter's niece, now the Empress Anna. Their Sich was re-established, albeit at another site. Bereft of their support, the weakened Khanate of Crimea was in dire straits.

In 1736, war again broke out between Russia and the Ottoman Empire. And once again the Cossacks served on the Russian side, if in a rather less loyal fashion: their own self-interest dictated a constant shift in local alliances, involving the other neighbouring peoples, not least the Poles and Don Cossacks. This attitude was especially evident in the following Russian-Ottoman War of 1769–74. To some degree they were alienated by Russia because of the latter's settlement policy, which imported immigrants to farm in the region to the north of Crimea, an activity the Cossacks were loath to carry out themselves, with the possible exception of animal husbandry. This culminated in the final abolition of the Zaporozhian Hetmanate by Russia in 1775, under the Empress Catherine the Great, and the flight of some 14,619 Cossacks to neighbouring Ottoman and Tatar lands. Their place was rapidly taken by Russians and other Slavs, including Old Believers (who rejected the Russian Orthodox Church reforms of the mid-seventeenth century) and ordinary soldiers.[32] By then, Russia's goals with respect to Crimea had already been achieved.

In 1768, Russia determined to secure permanent rights of navigation on the Black Sea and through the Bosporus Straits into the Mediterranean Sea. This required the establishment of a Russian naval port and for this Crimea was eminently suitable. At this stage Catherine the Great saw no need for conquest provided the integrity of the base was maintained. So when peace with the Sublime Porte was achieved by the Treaty of Küçük Kaynarca in 1774, Russia gained more than had been expected. A Black Sea coastal strip of modern Ukraine between the rivers Dniepr and Bug was ceded by the Sublime Porte to Russia. Most importantly, they secured the navigation rights to the Black Sea and beyond, as well as the Ottoman Crimean fortresses Yenikale and Kerch, both of which dominated the entrance to the Sea of Azov, adjacent to Russian territories acquired during the course of the eighteenth century. Crimea retained its independence, including its sovereignty over the Nogai Tatars to the east, but not for long. For the Ottomans and many Tatars, complete Russian hegemony in Crimea loomed on the horizon.

OTTOMAN ENCROACHMENT ON CRIMEA AND ITS RUSSIAN ANNEXATION

Growing Ottoman Domination of Crimea

From the middle of the seventeenth century, Ottoman encroachment and domination of the Khanate of Crimea increased significantly, reaching its apogee in the early eighteenth century. The Chronicle of Mehmed Giray (1704) relates the degree to which Crimea had by then become subordinate to the Sublime Porte. The sultan now appointed the khan himself and his own name was invoked first during Friday prayers in all the Khanate's mosques. That said, certain ancient rights from the foundation of the Khanate continued to be respected, namely the right of the Crimean khan to mint his own coins and the formal payment of tribute money, ubiquitous in all regions subject to the Ottomans, was never demanded. Other articles were seemingly mutual in scope: respect towards the subjects and property of each other's state, mutual assistance to be rendered according to need, as well as the obligation to engage in each other's battles against the infidel. None of these demands broke with tradition but this latter requirement of military assistance fell more upon Crimea than the Ottomans and most soured their relations.[1]

Under Khan Devlet II Giray's second reign (he ruled twice, from 1699–1702 and then from 1708–1713), matters deteriorated with respect to Crimean autonomy. In 1711, during the Turkish-Russian war in Moldavia, the Sublime Porte ignored Crimean demands to continue the war against Russian forces under Peter the Great, and ordered its Grand Vizier Baltacı Mehmed Pasha to conclude a humbling peace at Prut which, in the opinion of the khan, only benefited the Russians and disadvantaged the Crimeans. This was hardly mutuality.[2]

Russian Campaigns in Crimea

During the 1730s, new campaigns to extend Russian influence and power began again to focus on Crimea. In 1736, General Field Marshall Count Burchard Christoph von Münnich, a native of Oldenburg, then a duchy in today's Germany though in the employ of Russia, overran Ottoman defences in Crimea for the first time. Bakhchisaray was overrun by imperial Russian forces and the old palace of Bakhchisaray was destroyed. In consequence, he was awarded the Russian Imperial Order of the White Eagle, before defeating the Ottomans three years later at Stavuchany, near Khotyn, in today's Ukraine. This was the first successful attempt at undermining Ottoman hegemony on the peninsula, which would eventually lead to its complete annexation. Moreover, the increasing strengthening of the links between those inhabitants of Crimea who were not Tatar and Christian Europe further undermined Crimean Tatar hegemony. For example, the prominence of the Karaites there persisted during the eighteenth century. Their principal settlement was by now based at Chufut Kale and the culture they exerted was profoundly influential on the peninsula. Indeed, they established Crimea's first printing press there in 1734, when such a device was a rarity in Russia, thus linking them firmly with the wider global European world. It published at first using the Hebrew alphabet but later also used the media of Cyrillic and Latin, further strengthening bonds with Russia and elsewhere in Christian Europe.

For this and other reasons, therefore, during the 1760s, the Khanate of Crimea was by no means an Islamic realm hostile to Christian Europe or Europeans as such. On the contrary, the French Baron François de Tott was appointed an adviser to the Ottoman sultan, whilst also becoming French consul at the court of the Crimean khan Kirim Giray (d. 1769): indeed, he hunted, hawked and coursed with the latter, in the company not only of greyhounds but of his 6,000 cavalry men. Tott, moreover, assisted the khan, to the detriment of Russia, after the outbreak of the Russian-Turkish War. This took place not in Crimea but by the Polish-Bessarabian border in today's western Ukraine. There 100,000 Ottoman forces, including those from Crimea, opposed the Russians. However, the sudden death of the khan, under mysterious circumstances, led to a military hiatus, after the new khan Devlet IV Giray (1769–70 and 1775–77) ascended the throne.

Tott recorded the exotic magnificence of the ceremonial which attended this event, so at variance with military and political realities:

> Dressed in a cap loaded with two aigrettes enriched with diamonds, his bow and quiver flung across his body, preceded by his guards and several led horses whose heads were ornamented with plumes of feathers, followed by the standard of the Prophet and accompanied by all his Court, he repaired to his Palace where in the hall of the Divan, seated on his throne, he received the homage of all the grandees.[3]

The Russian-Turkish War raged from 1768 until 1774, and so for much of that period the Tatar army was not in Crimea. Consequently, in 1771, the Russian military leader Vasily Dolgoruky was able to attack and temporarily occupy the Khanate, and was only prevented by the serf rebellion of Pugachev from consolidating his gains. Nonetheless, Russia benefited from its conclusion, in July 1774, with the Treaty of Küçük Kaynarca. Indeed, its terms were highly unfavourable to the Porte, since it was forced not only to recognise Russia as guardian of the Christians of the Ottoman Empire – a fateful clause which would lead to the Crimean War and has implications in the Middle East to this day – but also because it recognised the independence of Crimea, albeit with the sultan still as caliph (supreme Islamic spiritual leader) of the Tatars. Moreover, not only was Russia now granted the nearby port of Kherson, on the Black Sea, west of Crimea, but Kerch itself in Crimea, as well as rights to the mercantile navigation on the sea. Greek Orthodox settlers were now not only permitted but encouraged to settle along Russia's new Black Sea littoral. An indemnity was to be paid and what is today the Ukrainian coast from the Dnieper River to the Bug was ceded to Russia, amongst other benefits. In consequence, civil strife erupted in Crimea amongst the pro-Ottoman factions who seemed to have frittered away Crimean interests in order to secure their own.

Şahin Giray (1745–87) who became Khan of Crimea in 1777, was a Hamlet-like figure, ambivalent and with a weak political will which boded ill for the future of the Khanate. Highly westernised, he had been educated in Venice, which, like the Ottoman Empire and the Khanate itself, was in rapid political and economic decline. Then, in 1771 he travelled to the St Petersburg court of Catherine the Great. The shrewd and manipulative empress was more impressed by the delicacy of his aesthetic tastes than his political acumen and used this to Russian advantage. As she wrote to

Voltaire, the philosophical pillar of the French Enlightenment: 'A sweet character, he writes Arabic poems...he's going to come to my circle on Sundays after dinner when he is allowed to enter to watch the girls dance ....'[4] When he departed for home, Catherine endowed him with 20,000 roubles and a gold sword, a small price to pay for her confidence that he would now support Russian interests when he eventually assumed the throne. In this she was right, for in 1783, after the Russian-Ottoman Treaty of Ainalikawak, unable to cope with Ottoman machinations which sought to undermine Crimean independence, Şahin Giray abdicated, transferring his rights of sovereignty to Catherine the Great and therefore Russia.

Leaving nothing to chance political vagaries, Grigory Potemkin, Russian military leader, governor of New Russia and possibly even the Empress's morganatic husband, had, in the meantime, settled Orthodox Christians in Crimea. Some 1,200 Greeks (known by contemporaries as Albanians) were brought over to the environs of Yenikale (in Tatar: New Fortress), which had been seized from the Ottomans who had constructed it from 1699–1706 specifically as protection against the Russians. This intrusion led to conflict with the Tatars, some of whom sought Ottoman assistance, not only against the Russians, but against their 'favourite', the Crimean khan himself. Şahin Giray fled and the Porte ordered his replacement, but Russian machinations secured his reinstatement. However, factionalism amongst the Tatars continued unabated, many of whom saw the Orthodox Christian settlers as the cause of their plight. Pogroms ensued and Russia intervened to secure the exodus of what was now almost 32,000 Christians – Greeks, Georgians and Armenians – into Russia itself. Altogether more than 22,000 Armenians emigrated from Crimea in 1778–1779, re-establishing themselves in New Russia, in Azov, Samara and in other settlements along the River Dnieper.

No less than General Alexander Suvorov, later hero of the Russian military campaign in Italy during the Napoleonic Wars, led the operation, with the assistance of Count Pyotr Rumiantsev-Zadunaisky. Like so many future forced exoduses of people from Crimea, this one proved disastrous and many died en route to Taganrog and the newly founded city of Mariupol, not from ill will, as would sometimes later be the case, but the parlous state of logistics.

The social and political order was rapidly deteriorating in Crimea and during this confusion Khan Şahin Giray fled for a second time, briefly replaced on the throne in the summer of 1783 by his pro-Ottoman brother Bahadir Giray. In response, then as now, Russia took matters into its own hands, with the support of the now de-throned Khan Şahin Giray. Potemkin met him on Russian territory at Petrovsk (today's Berdyansk), on the northern shores of the Sea of Azov. Thereafter, with the ex-khan's agreement, Russian forces under General Alexander Antonovich de Balmain marched into Crimea, capturing Bakhchisaray, the Tatar capital. Some 400 Tatar 'rebels' were killed, whilst Şahin Giray was once again placed upon his ancient throne. Most of the Tatar aristocracy then swore allegiance to Catherine the Great at Ak-Kaya (the White Cliff) near todays's Bilohirsk (in Tatar: Karasubazar). Potemkin, on his name day 30 September, was now in control of Crimea. His beloved Empress sent him costly presents and an understated message: 'What a wild place you've gone to for your name day, my friend.'[5]

Russian Annexation of Crimea

On 2 February 1784 the annexation of Crimea – thereafter known officially in Russia as the province of Taurida (using its old Greek name), with its population of some 140,000 – was finally achieved, justified internationally by the disorder reigning at the time. Now finally, what Potemkin styled the 'wart' on the nose of Catherine the Great, was lanced.[6] Shortly thereafter, on 8 April, an imperial manifesto was proclaimed giving a guarantee of religious toleration to the Crimean Tatars. Their lives, houses of worship and religious practices were all to be respected. In 1785, Tatar princes and nobles were also granted corresponding patents of Russian nobility, with privileged exemption from taxation and onerous services to the imperial government. Their property rights were also confirmed and, in some instances, enhanced by the granting of new estates. However, they were forbidden to own Christian serfs. Gradually, though, many became russified, even to the degree of adding Russian suffixes to their name or converting to Russian Orthodoxy.

The Muslim clergy, along with the nobility, were also required to take an oath of allegiance to the empress. In return, they were given a status similar to that of the Russian Orthodox clergy. The imperial administration passed edicts enabling a close supervision of training for the ulema (official scholars of Muslim Sharia law), even organising the translation and printing of various editions of the Qur'an through a Muslim state publishing house established in St Petersburg, which could be of use for all the Tatar peoples throughout the empire. In 1794, a special administrative body was established to supervise Muslim affairs in Taurida Province, under the auspices of the grand mufti, supreme Muslim leader in Crimea. He himself, though, was to be appointed by the tsar who, in return, granted him a patent of nobility and generous remuneration. Furthermore, the Islamic foundations and institutions, as well as the income from which they lived, were now also exempted from imperial taxation and other financial burdens. These measures helped to secure the loyalty, at this time, of a majority of Crimean clerics. Yet many thousands of Tatars over the following decades, indeed, century, became increasingly discontented and, whether for political, religious or other reasons emigrated across the Black Sea to the Ottoman Empire. It is said that some 20,000–30,000 refugees, Crimean and Nogai Tatars, left Crimea and other regions of Taurida Province, the majority supporters of Khan Şahin Giray.[7] The common Tatar peasant farmers, with few initial benefits, felt themselves even more disadvantaged. For, whilst protected from official legal serfdom and military service by imperial decree, they, nonetheless, often became de facto serfs in the sense that they were frequently obliged to provide their local landowners with as much as half of their harvest. This left them struggling to provide an existential minimum for themselves and their families, especially in times of hardship.

Christian settlers, on the other hand, now flocked to Crimea, in particular, Armenians, many of whom had abandoned their ancestral homesteads there under Muslim persecution only a few years before.

Establishment of the Sevastopol Naval Base

One of the first necessities of the new regime in Crimea was to establish a Black Sea naval base, of as much importance then for the exertion of Russian imperial authority in the Mediterranean as it is now. Already in June 1783, Potemkin had examined the harbour of Akhtiar, where a Tatar village was situated, and it was that site which was chosen. Since that time it has been known by its new Greek name Sevastapol. The noted Russian engineer Nikolai I. Korsakov was commissioned to carry out the fortifications and by the end of the decade it was and has remained Russia's most important naval base.

The new Russian capital of Taurida was established at the former Tatar town Ak-mechet, on the central plain, and was christened Simferopol. There a new city in the fashionable neo-classical, Greek inspired style, was constructed.

In May 1787, Catherine the Great herself, in the company of her ally the Emperor Joseph of Austria, visited Crimea, during a wider progress through New Russia. With great symbolism, she took up residence in the khan's former apartments at the Palace of Bakhchisaray. Along with a vast retinue of fearsome looking Cossacks and Tatar horsemen in glorious array, the empress was met by some two hundred 'Amazon warriors' – in reality, the wives of Russian military officers – exotically attired in crimson skirts and green jackets, both of velvet, but with fringes of gold, all crowned by white turbans and ostrich feathers, with spangles to add the sparkle.

Potemkin was elevated to the rank of field marshal by the empress because of his military successes which opened the doors to the expectation that Catherine the Great's greatest dream might be realised: it was common knowledge throughout Europe that Catherine had set her sights on Constantinople, from which she hoped to proclaim a new Byzantine Empire – the so-called Greek Project – under her grandson the Grand-duke Constantine, born in 1779, and named after the founder of the city, the Roman Emperor Constantine the Great. In hopeful expectation, that year, the Empress had silver coins minted in his honour depicting the Cathedral of Hagia Sophia, in Constantinople, functioning since the conquest as the capital's most important mosque. (Later as a boy, governesses from the Greek island of Naxos were brought to the Russian capital where they instructed Constantine in Greek, a language in which he became quite able.)

Ottoman Resistance to the Russian Annexation of Crimea

Needless to say, the Sublime Porte was outraged. In consequence, it declared war on Russia, joined by its allies Sweden and Poland, long time enemies of Russia. The Turks were also distressed that many of their former

Greek Orthodox who had emigrated from the Ottoman Empire to the Russian Black Sea coastal settlements were being encouraged to enlist in what they perceived as an anti-Ottoman campaign. Just before the commencement of hostilities, they lamented to the British envoy Sir Robert Ainslie, 'Subjects of this Empire who are induced to emigrate...already compose the major Part of the Mariners employed in the Russian Navy.'[8] Previously, only the strenuous exhortations of Britain and Hapsburg Austria had restrained the Ottoman Turks from going to war but in 1787 it erupted into what was for both sides a brutal conflict with many dead. It carried on until 1792, when the Treaty of Jassi (now Iasi, in north-eastern Romania) brought hostilities to a conclusion. This was a major defeat for the Ottomans. Crimea was left in Russian hands and Catherine the Great's vision, encouraged by Potemkin and the Zubovs (another love and his brother) had triumphed over that of Count Alexander Vorontsov, Russian ambassador to Great Britain, and the isolationists, who had rejected Russian imperialism. The publication by Russia's great court poet and statesman Gavrila Derzhavin in 1798 of a poem *The Waterfall*, written between 1791– 94, however, confirmed forever Potemkin's lofty status as the conquerer and founder of New Russia and its Crimean province of Taurida:

Art thou not he who put to flight
The mighty hordes of preying neighbours
And turned vast desert realms into
Cities and arable fields
And cloaked the Pontus Sea with ships
And shook the earth's core with thy thunder?

A number of Ottoman fortifications were relinquished to Russia after the peace. Surprisingly though, with respect to the exchange of prisoners which followed its conclusion, a number of Greek Orthodox captives who had fought for Russia (they had previously been privateers) objected to repatriation, in what a British diplomat labelled a 'scandalous and unexpected business'. As Will Smiley has put, 'the Ottomans eventually found themselves paying their captured subjects to agree to go and strengthen the Russian fleet, an outcome neither the captives, nor the Porte had desired. ... This incident revealed that for captives and states alike, the question of "who was an Ottoman" was complex and contested, but was also a matter of life and death, and of freedom and captivity.'[9]

The fate of Crimea, with its population of some 180,000,[10] was now conclusively determined: it became an integral part of New Russia and, as such, the Russian Empire. The annexation had, moreover, provided the tsar with a further 300,000 subjects, the overwhelming majority Tatars and Nogais, all of the Muslim faith.[11] For some of them, the future looked bright and many preferred the Russian imperial crown to the sultan's turban, for, after all, the Tatar peasants were confirmed in their personal and religious freedoms, under the protection of the tsar as 'state peasants', whilst many of the Tatar elite were confirmed in their noble status and property rights.

Alas, this upbeat future proved to be a chimera to many. Feeling their perceived rights, in the following years, intruded upon in a plethora of ways, some 100,000 Crimean Tatars – one third of their entire population – fled to the Ottoman Empire in the final decade of the eighteenth century. This flight was further exacerbated by the Russo-Turkish War of 1806–12, which led to the exile of a further 10,000 Crimean Tatars. To take their place, Christian colonists were shipped from the Ottoman Empire – an early form of ethnic cleansing – especially Greeks, Bulgarians and Armenians.[12] In the 1790s, their numbers had been small, only about 11,000, but this increased dramatically over the following decades.[13] For these Christians, those born both high and low – by contrast to the Crimean Tatar population itself – the future looked bright. Agriculture, trade and the arts were all given a high priority. Prince Grigory Potemkin himself even ensured the re-establishment of vineyards and the production of wine in Crimea after a centuries-long hiatus. The first half of the new century, therefore, witnessed a revival of Crimean agriculture, literary life, architecture and culture under Russian rule to a degree not experienced since classical times.

THE CONSOLIDATION OF CRIMEA
UNDER RUSSIAN CONTROL

Crimean Exoticism

By the early years of the nineteenth century, Russian control of Crimea had been successfully consolidated. With its stunning landscape and glorious almost semi-tropical weather, for half the year it increasingly became the playground for Russia's well-heeled nobility and effervescent intellectuals, captivated, in aesthetic terms, by its Islamic past.

It was Alexander Pushkin (1799–1837), Russia's most famous and beloved poet, who especially appreciated Crimea. Forbidden from travelling to European destinations outside Russia, Crimea became for him the closest substitute (once he was able to afford the trip from his internal exile in Odessa). It offered him the freedom, exoticness, sophistication and balmy charm which nowhere else in Russia could provide. It was also he who best captured the exotic nature of Tatar Crimea through his poem *The Fountain of Bakhchisaray* (1823), with its tragic tale of unrequited love. He himself was no less exotic and his very background was the stuff of fantasy – the great-grandson on his mother's side of Abram Gannibal, an Ethiopian slave boy, given as a gift to Peter the Great and eventually elevated to the Russian nobility. Some of Pushkin's own descendants settled in England and include cousins of Queen Elizabeth II and the current Duchess of Westminster. And Pushkin's end was no less dramatic – killed in a duel at the height of his literary and physical powers, in which the beauty of his aristocratic wife was a key element.

The Polish poet Adam Mickiewicz (1798–1855), who often visited Yevpatoria, also popularised the charms and exoticism of Crimea, based on his experiences exploring its numerous places of cultural interest. He too visited the Palace of Bakhchisaray, and even stayed in the rock dwellings of the non-Talmudic Jewish Karaite sect in the nearby mountain village of Chufut Kale, shortly before the Karaites themselves resettled at Yevpatoria.

It is said to have been at Simferopol, the capital of Crimea, that Mickiewicz first met the Russian dramatist and diplomat Alexander Griboyedov, famed for his humorous play *Woe from Wit*. The latter, a member of the Decembrists, a revolutionary group in the Russia of the late 1820s which sought to implement liberal values into the political system, who introduced Mickiewicz to the Polish man of letters and Polish nationalist, Gustaw Olizar, at a time when the divided country was parcelled out amongst Russia, Prussia and Austria. Mickiewicz stayed for a short period with Olizar at his villa of Cardiatricon (Heart's Remedy), situated on the Ayu Dagh promontory overlooking the Black Sea. For all the conspiratorial character of this intellectual circle, however, it remained a highly aristocratic one as well, including such court notables as the Princess Golitsyna. So incestuous was this circle that both Olizar and Pushkin vied for the same lady, the famous beauty Maria Rayevskaya, daughter of Russian General Nikolay Rayev. She eventually married Major General Prince Sergey Volkonsky – an even more notorious Decembrist as far as Tsar Nicholas I was concerned – who was later exiled to Siberia for his plotting, an exile the princess famously shared with him for over thirty years. Mickiewicz went on to write some eighteen Crimean sonnets, which were published together as a collection in 1826, to great international acclaim.

Religious Romanticism and Veneration of the Past

If an exotic romanticism came to dominate literary perceptions of Crimea, so too did religious romanticism, glorifying the ancient origins of Russian Orthodoxy, at that time (and perhaps even now) deemed one of the three pillars of the Russian state. In this respect, the most important site for historical veneration was Chersonesus. Here, by imperial order, archaeological excavations were undertaken in 1827, on the site of the Church of St Vladimir, said to be the location of the latter's conversion to Orthodox Christianity, when he was Great Prince of Kiev more than 800 years before.

Later, in 1850, Archbishop Innokenty (Borisov, 1800–57), leading ecclesiastic of the Russian Orthodox Church in Crimea, also sponsored an initiative which sought to restore ancient Orthodox churches and monasteries in the Crimean Mountains. His goal was to create a Russian equivalent of Mount Athos, that semi-autonomous Orthodox ecclesiastical region located on the Chalkidiki Peninsula of northern Greece, still thriving today.[1] Other monastic houses on the coast were also restored and enlarged at Inkerman, Chersonesus and Balaklava, in particular, the great Dormition Monastery. The site of the Cosmos and Damian spring, renowned for its healing waters, north of Alushta, was also developed, all of which increasingly attracted large numbers of pilgrims, many seeking spiritual rejuvenation, others bodily reinvigoration, still others just a good time. These endeavours, in many ways, can be seen as the beginnings of the establishment of the south of Crimea as a health resort for all of Russia, especially those suffering from lung complaints, in particular, tuberculosis, which has seen a resurgence throughout the former Soviet Union in recent years.

Innokenty was, of course, a devout Orthodox prelate but at the same time he was by no means anti-Tatar. It was Islam he was keen to contain and his principal spiritual goal in Crimea was to convert them. To this end, therefore, he encouraged the teaching of the Crimean Tatar language as a medium of conversion. Indeed, it became a subject at the Russian Orthodox Seminary in Odessa, which trained priests for all of New Russia, including Crimea. For those not amenable to conversion, however, life became more difficult.

As the Orthodox Church's privileges increasingly came to be promoted and extended in Crimea, so Muslim Tatars found themselves increasingly circumscribed in their worship and cultural life. Now only their old capital of Bakhchisaray and city of Karasubazar remained official Tatar enclaves. Feodosia and Yevpatoria, formerly important urban Crimean Tatar settlements, were russified and the Muslim population dwindled.

Count Mikhail Vorontsov

The most important political and cultural figure in Russian Crimea during the first half of the nineteenth century was, of course, not a Crimean Tatar but a Russian – Count Mikhail Semyon Vorontsov (1782–1856). A renowned military commander during the Napoleonic Wars, in which Russia and Britain were allied against Napoleonic France, he led the Russian cavalry which opposed Napoleon's invasion of Russia in 1812, an event later commemorated in Tschaikovsky's *1812 Overture*. Vorontsov himself saw action at the Battles of Borodino and Leipzig and later went on to crush resistance (1844–53) to Russian's imperial project in the Caucasus, for which he was eventually elevated to princely rank.

In 1823, Vorontsov was appointed governor-general of New Russia, including Taurida Province, and remained in this office until 1854. Keenly aware of the importance of modern technological developments, he introduced steamboats to Russia's Black Sea ports in 1828. His wife: Countess Elizaveta Vorontsova (née Branicka) was another great beauty who formed a liaison with Pushkin, when the latter was in internal exile in Odessa (the newly founded capital of New Russia), and inspired much of his most beautiful poetry. But Vorontsov himself had greater matters to attend to, including keeping the plague, which periodically raged in the Ottoman Empire, away from New Russia and Crimea. He also had to keep Ottoman military forces at bay during the Russo-Turkish War (1828–29). In 1856, the final year of the Crimean war, he was elevated to Russia's highest military rank, Field Marshal but by that stage was active in the Caucasus, rather than Crimea.

Vorontsov was also a great patron of architecture and the arts in Crimea – as well as in Odessa – and set about acquiring large tracts of land, on the south-western coastal strip of the peninsula, purchasing it from owner Colonel Theodosios Reveliotis, a pillar of the Greek community long resident in Crimea. These included estates at Alupka, Livardia and Oreanda, which he added to that already bought at Massandra, where he proceeded to construct not only some of Europe's most beautiful palaces, but to further the re-establishment of viniculture, as begun in the previous century by Prince Grigory Potemkin. In this he was assisted by other local notables, amongst them, one Joseph Blanc, who established himself at Sunny Valley, to the east of Sudak.

The Alupka Palace

First and foremost amongst the palaces built by Vorontsov was that of Alupka, built over a twenty-year period from 1828 to 1848 as a Russian dacha. Yet the architect was British – Edward Blore who also worked on Buckingham Palace – with the assistance of William Hunt. Costing over nine million silver roubles, it was the queen of all dachas ever built in Russia, its eclectic design, incorporating elements of English Gothic and Renaissance Revival Styles, Scottish Baronial and Indian architecture, in the spirit of the Brighton Pavilion. The employment of British architects was hardly a novelty in Russia – Catherine the Great had employed Cameron at the Imperial Palace of Pavlovsk and also for garden pavilions and such at Tsarskoe Celo, both near St Petersburg. But there was another link to Britain for Vorontsov: his uncle had been ambassador to the Court of St James during the late eighteenth century and his sister Ekaterina Semyonovna Vorontsov had married George Herbert, 11th Earl of Pembroke. Alas, this relationship did not prevent his nephew, the British Minister of War, Sidney Herbert, from bombarding the palace of his uncle in 1856, during the Crimean War. Fortuitously, however, Alupka survived and at the turn of the twentieth century would be immortalised in a poem by Ivan Bunin His poem *Long alley leading down to the shore* (1900) looks back at aristocratic life in the Russian countryside with an idealised nostalgia. Yet even then its heyday had long passed, the old Russia wiped out by the emancipation of the serfs in 1861 and the collapse of agriculture in the 1870s, a by-product of cheaper American agricultural imports.

In 1837, Tsar Nicholas I and his family visited Alupka and were so taken by its majesty and lush semi-tropical gardens that the Autocrat of all the Russias determined to build his own summer palace at nearby Oreanda, named after an alluring nymph in Classical Greek mythology. At first, Prussia's most famous neo-classical architect of the period, Karl Friedrich Schinkel, in Berlin, was appointed to carry out the work. However, his grandiose plans and the expense – too much even for the Tsar – brought an end to the project. Instead, the noted Russian architect but more modestly priced Andrey Schtakenschneider, famous for the neo-classical Mariinsky Palace, on St Isaac's Square and the neo-Rococo Beloselsky-Belosersky palaces, on the Fontanka River, both in St Petersburg, was commissioned to carry out the work. Built from 1842–52, in a late neo-classical style, it was destroyed by a fire in 1882 and never rebuilt. However, today one of Yalta's finest hotels, built in 1948, receives guests under the old name and the alluring summer charm of Oreanda still lives on in Chekhov's famous short story, *The Lady with the Dog*, published in 1899.

Livadia Palace

The most famous of these splendid palatial residences is the Livadia Palace, noted more for the important political events that took place there than for its architectural beauty. The land was first acquired from Count Semyon Vorontsov by the noble Polish Potocki family, but thereafter entered into the possession of Tsar Alexander II in the 1860s. At that time the Italian architect Ippolito Monighetti constructed an imposing palace complex there, including an Orthodox chapel, which became a favourite dacha of the imperial family. After the latter's assassination, Alexander III frequented the estate at various times of year, but preferred to live in an adjacent smaller pavilion where he died in November 1894. When Tsar Nicholas II assumed the throne, most of the palace complex was torn down in order to build an even more elaborate residence, suitable for its growing importance as a year round imperial residence, with no less than 116 rooms. In consequence, the Russian architect Nikolai Krasnov was commissioned to construct a palace in the Italian Renaissance style, but with other eclectic elements, enabling each facade to be distinctly individuated. The process took seventeen months and opened on the sixteenth birthday of his youngest daughter, the Grand Duchess Olga, on 11 September 1911. Its principal facade is graced by an arched portico of Carrara marble, and the windows evince the influence of the Italian Renaissance architect Bramante. Its interior boasts a Pompeian entrance hall and there is also a Florentine tower, with a belvedere, and terraces carried out in both Italianate and Islamic styles. English elements, beloved of Nicholas II, include a Victorian style billiard-room and Jacobean panelled study.

In the wake of the first Revolution, in February 1917, the Danish born Dowager Empress Maria Feodorovna, mother of Nicholas II and sister of Britain's Queen Alexandra, fled there, with other members of the imperial family, and remained, even after the Bolsheviks assumed control, until finally evacuated with them by the British naval ship HMS Marlborough, by order of her royal sister.

Later, in the Soviet period, Stalin came to stay there during the summer, but during the Second World War, it was occupied by the Germans, before it became the venue of that iconic meeting, the world famous Yalta Conference, where Stalin, Churchill and Roosevelt gathered to negotiate the post-war international settlement. After the re-establishment of Soviet authority and the end of the war, like so many palaces and stately homes in Russia, it was given over to become a psychiatric hospital. Finally, just before the fall of the Soviet Union (Gorbachev was on holiday in Crimea in August when a failed coup erupted in Moscow against him) and the subsequent independence of Ukraine, it was opened to the public as a museum and cultural venue. Indeed, the Ukrainian pop singer Sofia Rotaru performed and celebrated her sixtieth birthday at the palace in 2008, together with the Russian, Ukrainian and Moldavian heads of state, and funds from the event paid for its restoration. Built by Monighetti in 1866 from white Crimean granite in the Neo-Renaissance style, with a gallery connecting it to the neo-Byzantine Church of the Exaltation of the Cross, it remains one of Crimea's leading international showcases.

Melas Palace

Another striking stately edifice is the Melas Palace built during the Napoleonic Wars for Count L. Perovsky, a Russian hero of 1812. It has a Moorish style, but with a classical garden folly overlooking the coast which was designed as a ruined Greek temple in the form of a semi-rotunda, by the British architect Philip Elson (1785–1867), in 1834. From 1856–75 the palace became the residence of the Russian poet, novelist and playwright Aleksey Tolstoy (1817–75), best known for his folk ballad *Vasily Shibanov*, published in 1858, about the time of Ivan the Terrible in the late sixteenth century. After his death, Princess Daria Golitsyna resided there during the summer months until 1885, although old Prince Golitsyn had already built his palace at Gaspra in 1836. More commonly known as Princess Moustache because of her hairy overlip, she served as the model for Pushkin's elderly, autocratic character, the Queen of Spades, in his renowned tragic novel, later turned into one of the greatest operas of the same name, by the composer Piotr Tchaikovsky (1840–93). Thereafter, the palace changed hands twice and, in the wake of the Revolution and the occupation of Crimea by the Bolsheviks, Melas was nationalised, becoming a sanatorium during and after the Soviet period.

Governor Naryshkin's Mansion

Moving inland to the suburbs of Simferopol, an anomaly in an otherwise drab architectural landscape, is Stilgirka, a charming Greek Revival mansion, adorned by a simple Doric portico, surmounted by a plain freeze, with gabled pavilions at either end, the broad steps leading to the entrance guarded by fearsome stone lions on elevated plinths. This is the former residence of Crimean Governor Dimitry Naryshkin, a descendant of the great Muscovite boyar family from which Peter the Great's mother, Natalia, issued. Originally the estate, situated in the Salgirka Park, had belonged to the famed German biologist and zoologist Peter Simon Pallas but construction of the mansion began in 1826, two years after it was acquired from his widow. The architect here, too, was Philip Elson. However, in 1834, Mikhail Semenovich Vorontsov acquired it and, in 1837, he hosted the imperial family itself, as well as the noted poet and Tutor to Crown Prince Alexander, the future Tsar Alexander II, Konstantin Zhukovsky. The renowned French traveller and scientist Dubois de Monpere also visited that same year, just one of many highly educated and imminent personages to grace its halls, with discussions of the latest scientific theories and discoveries. It also boasted a large garden folly, the Bakhchisaray Pavilion, in the Tatar style, crowned by minarets, also designed by Elson.

The Romantic Landscape Paintings of Crimea

Whilst a Golden Age of Architecture was achieved in Crimea during the nineteenth century, a similar one with respect to Russian romantic landscape paintings also thrived there, glorifying the beauties of the region's extraordinary mountains and hanging gardens.

Amongst the most famous painters was the Russian Nikanor Chenetsov (1805–1879) who had studied at the Russian Imperial Academy of Art in St Petersburg, winning the Gold Medal in 1827. He was invited to Crimea by invitation of Count Vorontsov himself, who was leading member of the Society for the Encouragement of Artists, in order to depict the beauty of his gardens at Alupka. Chenetsov also produced a series of Crimean landscape paintings of great charm in the 1830s which became highly popularised lithographs throughout Europe in the following decades.

Political Friction

Unfortunately, the delights of Crimea's cultural life did not spill over into the international political arena of that time. Already in 1828, Colonel George de Lacy Evans, later serving as a general in charge of the 2nd Infantry Division of the British Army during the Crimean War, published a pamphlet, *On the Designs of Russia*, full of ominous warnings. It focused upon the spectre of Russian military aggrandisement against the Ottoman Empire, the real aim of which was not only the conquest of the Balkans but Ottoman Asia Minor, thereby also undermining British authority and trade with India.

As for Persia, it too was perceived as a threat, because 'Herat, in the hands of Persia', as a British ambassador put it, 'can never be considered in any other light than as an advanced *point d'appui* for the Russians toward India.'[2]

As Henry Temple, 3rd Viscount Palmerston wrote to Lord John Ponsonby in December 1833:

> No reasonable doubt can be entertained that the Russian Government is intently engaged in the prosecution of those schemes of aggrandisement towards the South which, ever since the reign of Catherine, have formed a prominent feature of Russian policy.

He further expounded:

> The cabinet of St Petersburg, whenever its foreign policy is adverted to, deals largely in the most unqualified declarations of disinterestedness; and protest that, satisfied with the extensive limits of the empire, it desires no increase of territory, and has renounced all those plans of aggrandisement which were imputed to Russia…

> But notwithstanding these declarations, it has been observed that the encroachments of Russia have continued to advance on all sides with a steady march and a well-directed aim, and that almost every transaction of much importance, in which of late years Russia has been engaged, has in some way or

other been made conducive to an alteration either of her influence or of her territory.[3]

Palmerston translated these words into actions in so far as he gave permission to Ponsonby to send part of the British fleet into the Mediterranean, should a Russian attack on Constantinople seem imminent.

France, too, was increasingly assuming a hostile position vis-à-vis Russia. A French publication *La Russie en 1839*, analysing Russia in depth over some six editions, proved so popular that it was republished in a variety of languages, including English, German and Danish, as well as in an abridged form in a number of other European languages.[4]

Mercantile Friction

British friction with Russia in the 1830s was not restricted to the political and military spheres; there was also a mercantile dimension. Ukraine was for centuries the breadbasket of Russia and vast quantities of grains were exported through the ports of Odessa, Taganrog and elsewhere to the west and east of Crimea in New Russia. British merchants were thus in open competition with the cosmopolitan middle men of this region – a battle they would eventually lose as, later in the century, Ukrainian grain flooded into Britain overwhelming such imports from everywhere else.

Visit of Tsar Nicholas I to Britain

In an attempt to improve relations, Tsar Nicholas I determined on a visit to Britain. His late brother Tsar Alexander I had come there on a state visit in June 1814, an event which had proved to be a high point in British-Russian relations. However, at this time his older brother had been seen as a progressive figure, whilst Nicholas was already tainted in the press as a tyrant. Hostile to revolutionaries of all persuasions – even pan-Slavic ones – he despised liberalism. He wrote, with respect to the seditious Russians who sought to bring all 'brother' Slavs together into a unitary state:

> they conceal the rebellious idea of union of those tribes, despite their legitimate citizenship in neighbouring and allied states, and they expect this to be brought about not through God's will but from the violent attempts that will make for the ruin of Russia herself.[5]

This visit, however, was less formal than that of Alexander, for the tsar arrived 'incognito' as Count Orlov, a fairly transparent ruse which enabled him and his entourage much greater freedom of movement and protocol. Arriving at Woolwich on a vessel bearing the Dutch flag, he was greeted by the Russian ambassador to the Court of St James's, Baron Brunov, with whom he took up residence at Ashburnham House (now a part of Westminster School), a stone's throw from Westminster Abbey, in London. The following day he was received by the young Queen Victoria at Buckingham Palace.

A highlight of his travels was a visit to a race meeting at Ascot, in which the Gold Cup was rechristened the Emperor's Cup in his honour (it would revert to its former name in the wake of the Crimean War). Handsome and affable, he made a favourable impression on most people, surprisingly even Lord Melbourne, during a breakfast at Chiswick House. As for his relations with the government itself they seemed to be highly satisfactory at the time. Indeed, Nicholas was convinced that Peel and Lord Aberdeen were sympathetic to Russia, not least with respect to his plans vis-à-vis the Ottoman Empire and its eventual dismemberment. This would prove to be a calamitous misunderstanding.[6]

It was later compounded, after the re-establishment of the French Empire under Napoleon III following a plebiscite in November 1852, for this evoked a widespread European unease, as fears of a new territorially aggressive France spread to the four corners of the continent. Indeed, Lord Raglan, later to lead British forces in the Crimean War, was preoccupied in 1852 –53 with strengthening British and, in particular, London's defences for this reason.

Nonetheless, out of a corner of its eye, the British government was still wary of the Russians, as much if not more so than the French. After all, the Russian army had increasingly been hemming in the Chechnyan leader, Imam Shamil of Gimry, in the latter phase of the Caucasus War (1817–64), with ever greater reinforcements, under their commander-in-chief Count Mikhail Vorontsov, the governor-general of New Russia and viceroy of the Caucasus now under Russian sovereignty. This, to many in Britain, posed a threat to India.

Armenian Community

Crimea was by now becoming a Russian province with an ever-growing Slavic population, but there was another Christian people who played an increasingly prominent role – the Armenians. The Armenian Community of Crimea thrived during this first half of the nineteenth century, as their mercantile networks grew and as conditions worsened in Ottoman Armenia itself. Without doubt its most prominent figure in Crimea was the noted marine painter Ivan Aivazovsky (1817–1900), who was born and died in Feodosia. His paintings today fetch vast sums on the international art market and a museum dedicated to his memory, the National Picture Gallery of Feodosia, boasts a splendid collection of his works. However, the Armenian community was a fractious one, divided into opposition groups along religious lines. One such internal squabble occurred in 1842 when, the Armenian Catholicos of Crimea was deposed from authority over the Armenian Apostolic Church, the leadership of which transferred to a new Chief Guardian.

Growing Russian Emigration

Russia was by now changing the life and culture of Crimea, not by political enactments or force of arms but by immigration. By mid-century, Crimea was increasingly populated by Russians, who had grown to number more than 70,000 out of a total population of 250,000. Improved roads and transport infrastructure helped to encourage this immigration, in particular, the construction of a coastal road from Sevastopol to Yalta in 1848, from which roads and later the railways extended northwards throughout the Russian Empire. The Crimean Tatars, by contrast, although still the majority in Crimea were suffering a serious demographic decline, down from 90 to 60 per cent, the 30 per cent having emigrated as refugees to its former ally the Ottoman Empire.[7] However, it was the following decade which wrought a greater havoc in Crimea than the province had known since the arrival of the Tatars centuries before.

THE CRIMEAN WAR

Roots of the Crimean War

The Middle East has always been a powder keg of inter-religious conflict, not only amongst Christians, Jews and Muslims, but amongst Christian communities themselves, each viewing the other as schismatic or heretical. And it was one such violent and deadly commotion that broke out on Good Friday 1846 (both the Julian and Gregorian calendars celebrated the same day that year) between Catholic and Orthodox Christians in the Church of the Holy Sepulchre, in Jerusalem. Forty of the faithful – the faithful of both of these then hostile communities – died in the slaughter. For Russia, seeing itself as the Third Rome – the inheritor of the Byzantine Empire, the second Rome – and the country with the world's largest Orthodox population, it was a matter of religious duty to come to their aid. After all, some 15,000 Russian pilgrims visited the site each year, a minority travelling hundreds, some even thousands, of kilometres on foot.[1] So Russia took matters into its own hands.

There were, moreover, other dimensions to the conflict: Russia wished to expand its political, territorial and economic interests not only in the Balkans, Caucasus and Middle East, but also in Central Asia – the gateway to Afghanistan and British India. This did not go unnoticed by the western colonial powers. Already in the early 1840s, William Young, British consul in Ottoman Jerusalem, had reported to the Foreign Office that there was a growing presence of 'Russian agents', who were preparing the 'Russian conquest of the Holy Lands'. He was convinced, as secularly minded people usually are, that this was being done under the pretence of Orthodox religious devotion, in particular, through the ever increasing numbers of Russian pilgrims travelling south and through sponsored pilgrimages and the purchases of land for new Orthodox churches and monasteries.[2] It was in this context that the ancient Orthodox Dormitian Monastery near Bakhchisaray, in Crimea, the origins of which were medieval, was also rebuilt in the 1850s (during the 1990s it underwent a major restoration in not dissimilar circumstances).

In France, the religious dimension alone was enough to raise French hackles, for traditional Catholics, clerics and laymen, viewed Orthodoxy with hostility, in particular, the French Ambassador to the Sublime Porte, Charles, Marquis de LaValette. It was he who, bolstered by papal support, maintained the rights of the French to protect all Christians in the Ottoman Empire and found a willing mouthpiece for his views in the important *Journal des débuts*. Needless to say, Tsar Nicholas I felt himself increasingly hemmed in by the western powers, hostile spiritually as well as militarily to Russia, and issued further ominous threats to the French and the Ottomans. In no way was he, emperor of the Third Rome, prepared to sacrifice the ten million Orthodox, of numerous ethnicities under Ottoman hegemony, to what he perceived as Islamic and Roman Catholic oppression.[3] After all, even the highly Eurastian and secularised Peter the Great, from whom he was descended, had, after defeating the Ottomans in 1699, asserted what he felt to be his rights as defender of the Orthodox in general and Russians in particular in the Ottoman Empire, and, not least, their access of pilgrimage to the Holy Land.

1853 – Preliminaries to the Outbreak of War

The Russian occupation of the Danubian principalities was the immediate trigger to the conflict, threatening the Ottoman Empire's Balkan provinces. Yet at the time of its occurrence, many amongst the Allies were not alarmed. Indeed, some even saw it as justified. Lord Aberdeen, the British prime minister, was one such and saw no grounds to engage in military confrontation. He felt that the Russians did have special rights in Ottoman Palestine to protect Christians and so preferred a diplomatic solution. Indeed, in February 1853, he admonished Lord Russell not to send the British fleet to the aid of the Ottomans. He wrote of the Turks:

> These Barbarians hate us all, and would be delighted to take their change of some advantage, by embroiling us with the other Powers of Christendom. It may be

necessary to give them our moral support, and to endeavour to prolong their existence; but we ought to regard as the greatest misfortune any engagement which compelled us to take up arms for the Turks.[4]

Soon, however, the pacific views of Lord Aberdeen were thrown aside in the opprobrium which was cast upon Russia and its ruler by the British and French press. To the Russians this was a slap in the face. Mikhail Pogodin in whose writings the tsar found a resonance for his own views, wrote of what he perceived to be an extraordinary level of western European hypocrisy, in particular with respect to the British and French in their own colonial wars:

> France takes Algeria from Turkey, and almost every year England annexes another Indian principality: none of this disturbs the balance of power; but when Russia occupies Moldavia and Wallachia, albeit only temporarily, that disturbs the balance of power. France occupies Rome and stays there several years in peacetime: that is nothing; but Russia only thinks of occupying Constantinople, and the peace of Europe is threatened. The English declare war on the Chinese, who have, it seems, offended them: no one has a right to intervene; but Russia is obliged to ask Europe for permission if it quarrels with its neighbour.[5]

By a strange quirk of political history, it was left to Sidney Herbert, second son of the Earl of Pembroke, the British Secretary at War from 1852–55, to cope with the Danubian principalities, Crimea and the prospect of war, in spite of the fact that he was the nephew of the latter province's governor-general Count Mikhail Vorontsov, who had served as a general in the Napoleonic Wars, as well as in the Russian-Turkish War (1828–29), in which Russia had been pitted against the Ottomans. Herbert's mother Catherine was, as previously discussed, the daughter of the former Russian ambassador Count Semyon Vorontsov, but close family relationships such as these – just as in the First World War – in no way mitigated the march to war, nor its severity. Neither did a sudden softening of the belligerent stance taken by Russia, for when Russian forces finally agreed to retreat from the Balkan principalities, the British cabinet decided to pursue a military solution in Crimea anyway. This, they determined, could only be resolved by Russia's acceptance of the so-called Four Points, formally laid down on 8 August by Britain, France, the Ottomans and Austria, after several months of negotiations.

American military or logistical support for western European countries was still unheard of. There was therefore neither a 'special relationship' to rely on, nor any solidarity in times of war. Whilst it is true that diehard abolitionist Republicans in the north states tended to favour Britain, other northerners, especially in the military, did not. George B. McClellan, a Major-General for the Union forces during the American Civil War, for example, actually travelled to Russia where he became an adviser to the Russian military – he saw the importance of muskets over bayonets in modern military engagements. Numerous American volunteers also joined the Russian side, including some forty medical doctors who assisted in the battle zone.[6] Others, such as Samuel Colt, the Connecticut born inventor of the Colt revolver, introducer of interchanging parts for weapons, and armaments manufacturer, sold arms and ammunition to both sides, presenting both the tsar and the sultan with gold-plated versions of the Colt, the former now on display in the Hermitage, St Petersburg, the other in the Metropolitan Museum of Art, New York City.

As for the Democrats of the South, they certainly did not sympathise with Britain. They felt that Russia shared a kindred spirit and also understood how a society with vast numbers of bonded labour functioned. With many citizens of Irish and French origin, a significant proportion of the southern white population still looked on Britain as an old enemy who, if it became ever more powerful, might once again attack their freedoms.

Yet there was one more pragmatic reason for the United States government to assist the Russians: the desire to purchase Russian America, that is, Alaska. Negotiations began at this time, even if it took until 1867 for the transfer of the Russian territory to the United States. Thus, in 1853, it was the failure of Russia to accept the following four demands which was decisive in the outbreak of war:

The Four Point Ultimatum to Russia

1. Russia should renounce any protection rights in Serbia and the Danubian principalities, these to be taken over by the Porte itself, albeit guaranteed by the other Allies.
2. The River Danube to be open to the merchant vessels of the world.

3. The Straits Convention of 1841 revised to put an end to Russia's naval domination of the Black Sea, 'in the interests of the Balance of Power in Europe'.
4. The Russian claim to protect the Christian subjects of the Ottoman Empire to be henceforth shared jointly with Britain, France and Austria in concert with the Turks themselves.[7]

These points rejected by Russia, the brink of war was now reached.

Opening of Hostilities

With trouble brewing in the ever-weakening Ottoman Empire and France endeavouring to assert the authority of the Roman Catholic Church with respect to the Holy Christian Sites of Palestine, war had become inevitable. Russia saw itself as coming to the defence of Orthodoxy, for which, as the Third Rome, it saw itself as protector, aside from any political or territorial benefits to be achieved, both of which were also significant.

On 28 March 1854, the Crimean War broke out, a conflict which would last for over two years, between Britain, France, Sardinia and the Ottoman Empire, on one side, and huge but isolated Russia, on the other. However, with respect to Britain and France, the assault began in earnest on 22 April, Orthodox Easter Sunday, when they commenced a bombardment of the capital of New Russia, Odessa, after its local governor, General Count Dimitry Osten-Sacken, had been confronted with an ultimatum to surrender his ships, which had gone unheeded. The allied fleet shelled the elegant neo-classical city for almost half a day, leaving a trail of destruction – Count Vorontsov's palace was hit along with the Hotel London and there were dozens of casualties.

At the opening of hostilities the Russian Black Sea Fleet was a powerful force, composed of two naval squadrons. The squadron under Admiral Vladimir Kornilov monitored the western Black Sea region, that of Vice-Admiral Pavel Nakhimov, the eastern one. However, military command over both was invested in Prince Alexander Menshikov (1787–1869). His main priority was to prevent the Ottomans from supplying their Muslim allies in the Caucasus with weapons, where war against Russia had been going on for over three decades. Therefore, the Ottomans, in response, sent their own fleet to preserve their Black Sea supply roots to their rebellious co-religionists.

Russia had a powerful military, but as the largest country in the world, much of it was dispersed over its vast expanse. Of the 1.2 million Russian soldiers in the field, 260,000 were guarding the Baltic coast, 293,000 were in Poland and western Ukraine, 121,000 were in Bessarabia and along the Black Sea coast, whilst 183,000 were stationed in the Caucasus.[8]

The assault of the Russian navy upon the Ottoman fleet provided the casus belli of the Crimean War. This took place at Sinope on the north-central coast of Ottoman Anatolia on 30 November 1853 (the event would later be celebrated in a famous oil painting by the great Russian-Armenian maritime painter Ivan Aivazovsky). When news reached London on 11 December, the British press fell upon Russia as it would do many times again over the following century and a half: Russia was accused of atrocities and blamed – incorrectly – for the deaths of the some four thousand civilians.[9]

One of the few voices of cool reason and restraint was Queen Victoria herself. She privately wrote:

> We have taken on ourselves in conjunction with France all the risks of a European war without having bound Turkey to any conditions with respect to provoking it. The hundred and twenty fanatical Turks constituting the Divan at Constantinople are left sole judges of the line of policy to be pursued, and made cognisant at the same time of the fact that England and France have bound themselves to defend the Turkish territory. This is entrusting them with a power which Parliament has been jealous to confide even to the hands of the British Crown.[10]

There was, moreover, even in Britain a religious objection to siding with the Ottomans. After all, Anglican and Church of Scotland missionaries were forbidden to proselytise amongst the Muslims – only the Orthodox and Catholics had that right. Perhaps for that reason the evangelical militant Lord Shaftesbury, notwithstanding the Ottoman crushing of Greek revolts in Epirus and Thessaly, turned his religious wrath against the Orthodox hierarchy, both Greek and Russian, even more than against the Muslim authorities themselves. He found it a particular abomination that the Russian Bible was read in Old Church Slavonic translation from the original Hebrew and Greek and not in Russian (at this time only the psalms had been translated and a complete Russian translation of the Bible would take the following generation of scholars to achieve). Even without him, though, the British press's baying for Russian blood was at fever pitch. With a larger British newspaper reading public than ever before, this frenzied encouragement by the press was the most crucial reason for entering the conflagration which had erupted on the shores of the Black Sea, so far from home.

Napoleonic France was also waving the banners of war against Russia and with ever greater fervour. Indeed, in anticipation of the Entente's usage against the German Kaiser during the First World War, newspapers, such as the Impartial, were cursing Tsar Nicholas I as a modern-day Attila, leading Europe's latter-day Huns:

> To pretend otherwise is to overturn all notions of order and justice. Falsity in politics and falsity in religion – that is what Russia represents. Its barbarity, which tries to ape our civilisation, inspires our mistrust; its despotism fills us with horror... the policies of Nicholas have raised a storm of indignation in all the civilised states of Europe; these are the policies of rape and pillage; they are brigandage on a vast scale.[11]

As for the tsar, never a great one for compromise, he had already become entrenched in his convictions that only a military confrontation with the Porte, Britain and France would resolve the matter. On 16 February Russia withdrew its ambassadors from both the Court of St James's and the Tuileries. Only now did Napoleon III shift slightly, becoming mildly accommodating in proposing a quid pro quo solution with respect to the Danube principalities and the operation of fleets on the Black Sea. For Nicholas, however, this stopped short of resolving the immediate casus belli, the conveyance of military equipment on ships to the Caucasus by the Ottomans. Conflict could only be avoided, he proposed, if France and Britain would ensure that inspections of Ottoman ships which might conceivably be carrying military equipment to the Caucasus would be undertaken. This confirmation was not forthcoming and five days later the Tsar unequivocally rejected Napoleon III's proposals. A massive enlargement of the military confrontation was now to be expected.

On the Russian side, Nicholas felt deeply that God saw Russia as the defender of both the faith and Mother Russia itself. He confided in King Frederik Wilhelm of Prussia, in March 1854, that he was prepared without allies if need be to defend his country and forces against any British and French aggression:

> Waging war neither for worldly advantage nor for conquests, but for a solely Christian purpose, must I be left alone to fight under the banner of the Holy Cross and to see the others, who call themselves Christians, all unite around the Crescent to combat Christendom?… Nothing is left to me but to fight, to win, or to perish with honour, as a martyr of our holy faith, and when I say this I declare it in the name of all Russia.[12]

In London, Lord Aberdeen took a not altogether contrary viewpoint, Indeed, he lamented to Queen Victoria and her consort Prince Albert, on 26 March, two days before the British declaration of war, that he was being 'dragged into a war' by Palmerston, whose position was bolstered by the press and public opinion.[13] No doubt this was so, but if there was to be war it had to be carried out by all means, fair and foul.

Undermined at its Caucasian flank, Russia was also at a major disadvantage with respect to logistics and its military preparedness. Not only Britain and France, but Austria, too, threatened its western borders – the latter, feeling vulnerable, in turn, from possible assaults by newly independent Serbia, which hated the Habsburgs and stridently supported Russia. In consequence, Austria sent some 25,000 soldiers to reinforce its own eastern border.[14] But this was unnecessary, as of all the armies involved in the Crimean War, the Russian was the least professional, composed as it was predominantly of illiterate conscripted serfs and state peasants. That said, it did have the greatest numbers of troops, more than a million in the infantry alone, and a further quarter of a million irregulars, most of whom were Cossacks. A further three-quarters of a million reservists backed them up. However, training was generally poor and their equipment even worse, depending as they did at the beginning of the war on outmoded Russian-made muskets and bayonets. Only during its later course did the Russian military introduce rifles into general use.[15]

These circumstances notwithstanding, from the outset the Russians were optimistic, especially those who had not yet arrived at the front lines. The young Lev Tolstoy wrote to his aunt in early May from the Danubian Principalities:

While you are imagining me exposed to all the danger of war, I have not yet smelt Turkish powder, but am very quietly at Bucharest, strolling about, making music, and eating ice-creams.[16]

Russia Attacked on All Sides

The Crimean War went on to be fought on a wide variety of fronts, from the Kola Peninsula, abutting the Arctic Sea, in the Russian north, to the shores of the peninsula of Kamchatka off the eastern coast of Siberia, and the Finnish Åland Islands (prisoners-of-war from which were carried off to England) and the archipelago of Helsinki in the Baltic around the Fortress of Sveaborg (Suomenlinna today). Russia, the Allies felt, had to be attacked on all sides and, as Palmerston had advised the British Cabinet in March 1854, Russia would be permanently weakened through a victory which required not only that Crimea be ceded to the Ottoman Empire, but that Finland should be returned to Sweden, from which it had been ceded to Russia as an autonomous grand-duchy, during the Napoleonic Wars, in 1809. The British navy, for which the Russian one was no match, was felt to be just the tool necessary to accomplish this and with only a limited expenditure of men.

In 1855, when Austria, too, joined the allied military affray, Nicholas I felt betrayed. He was fully aware that it had been Palmerston's intention to transfer Russian Poland and Bessarabia to the Habsburgs. It is said that the portrait of the young Austrian Emperor Franz Josef which he had kept in his private quarters in St Petersburg was henceforth turned to the wall, on its back, two words scrawled by the tsar himself, 'You Ingrate'.[17]

If Russia felt threatened in the west, it was also threatened in the east. For whilst there were 183,000 men on active service in the Caucasus, the region was, then as now, in a state of simmering revolt.[18] Some amongst the Allies saw this as Russia's Achilles heel. For that reason, John Urquhart, a British special agent, was sent out to the Caucasus to encourage the Chechen leader Shamil to declare a jihad against Russia. The French, too, sent out their own man Charles Champoiseau, to encourage an insurgency amongst the Circassians in the environs of Sukhumi, in Georgia.[19]

Still not all was bleak for Russia. Its regular army was no mean force, consisting of some 980,000 trained men and well over a million soldiers and sailors were further inducted, including Cossacks, militia, raw recruits and serfs. But many of these could not be mobilised in Crimea, as they were needed in other parts of the empire under threat. Russian military technology was primitive compared to that of the Allies. Its financing had, in part, been secured through loans by the great banking house of Alexander Stieglitz whose father Ludwig had financed the early building of railways in Russia during the 1830s and early 40s. Inflation was also a problem and the amount of paper money put into circulation more than doubled. Furthermore, the transport infrastructure of the empire was dreadful, with only a limited system of railways and poor roads, often inundated by melting ice and water, which turned them to mud in the spring and autumn. Communications were even more appalling and the disparity between that of Russia and the Allies were shocking: communications to the latter's capitals were soon almost instantaneous by virtue of the telegraph. However, it still took St Petersburg over a week to receive news by courier from Crimea.

Landing at Yevpatoria

The Allies first landed on the mainland of Crimea at Yevpatoria, deemed a safe anchorage, on 14 September 1854. From a distance this cosmopolitan town – Crimean and Karaite Tatars, Armenians, Russians and Greeks made up its population of some nine thousand inhabitants – seemed to resemble Holland with its plethora of windmills. Indeed, like that country it was an important agricultural centre, in this case for wheat which was not merely exported from the port but also grown on the steppes which formed its hinterland. It also had good sources of water – a problem both then and now in most of Crimea.[20]

That it was a centre of Tatar life was a major advantage for the western allies, since both Crimean and Karaite Tatars often acted as a third column in Crimea, turning on the Russians as their local interests dictated. Since together they composed a majority of the peninsula's entire population, this was a major worry for the Russians and, indeed, many soldiers were attacked by Tatar bands even before they reached the Isthmus of Perekop which served as a Russian land bridge to Crimea. These soldiers took even greater fright when rumours spread that Ottoman forces were establishing themselves in Yevpatoria, amongst their Muslim Tatar brothers.

The Tatars

By 1854, the Tatars, after half a century of Russian colonisation, albeit reduced in numbers and increasingly swamped by Russian and other European settlers – still made up about 60 per cent of the entire Crimean population. It was for that reason that the Allies had induced Mussad Giray, a descendant of the Crimean khans, to come to Crimea to drum up western support amongst his fellow Tatars,[21] in particular, those in Yevpatoria, Feodosia and Perekop.

Yet the reality was that many Tatars, especially in the elite, supported Russia, volunteered and fought faithfully for the Tsar. One painting from this period, *Crimean Tatar Squadron Officers of Life Guards Cossack Regiment* by the German artist Carl Friedrich Schulz (1796–1866), commemorates those members of the Tatar elite who fought in the Crimean War. Tsar Nicholas I commissioned this work during the war for his palace at Tsarskoe Selo, outside St Petersburg.

That said, there was no denying anti-Russian feeling amongst some Tatars, both from the elite and even in the general population, which led many Russians in Crimea, in particular, those who were Orthodox, to look upon them with suspicion. This was particularly true of the Russian Orthodox Church's hierarchy and especially the leading churchman of Crimea during the war Archbishop Innokenty, who perceived them as a major threat both militarily and spiritually and preached to this effect from his pulpit.

Russian Response

The allies had largely been ignorant about the severity of the Crimean winter yet this very ignorance offered them one major advantage: the Russian Commander General Menshikov had not thought that they would be foolish enough to start a campaign at such an adverse time of year. Therefore, he himself was unprepared when the attack occurred and he had to make do with no more than the 38,000 soldiers and 18,000 sailors in the vicinity, backed up by a further 12,000 troops on the eastern coast by Kerch and Feodosia. Even Simferopol itself, the capital of Crimea, could only boast a single Russian military battalion for its protection.[22] This was hardly an auspicious beginning for the Russian defensive campaign.

Battle of the Alma

The first actual battle of the Crimean War was at the Alma on 20 September 1854. The Russian troops of Menshikov had established themselves on the Alma Heights, overlooking the road to Sevastapol to the south. It was from there that the Cossack Captain Robert Chodasiewicz left the following impressions:

> On reaching our position on the heights, one of the most beautiful sights it was ever my lot to behold lay before us. The whole of the allied fleet was lying off the salt lakes to the south of Yevpatoria, and at night their forest masts were illuminated with various coloured lanterns. Both men and officers were lost in amazement at the sight of such a large number of ships together, especially as many of them had hardly ever seen the sea before. The soldier says, "Behold, the infidel has built another holy Moscow on the waves", comparing the masts of the ships to the church spires of that city.[23]

Yet despite being on home territory, the Russians were at a numerical disadvantage, with only 35,000 Russian soldiers – albeit with in excess of 100 artillery field guns – pitted against some 60,000 Allied forces down below. Nonetheless, they were not unduly worried. Indeed, many ladies from Sevastopol joined the Russian officers to watch the military 'theatre'.[24] They were not disappointed with the drama.

The French forces, under the command of Bosquet, who had joined in the assault, included the Zouaves Regiment, principally composed of colonial troops from Algeria, conquered about thirty years before from the Algerine tributary of the Ottomans. Highly agile, and famous for their skills in using trees to scale cliffs, they proved lethal to the defending Moscow Regiment which tried to fend them off until further reinforcements had arrived.[25]

When the Russian forces were defeated at Alma towards the end of that day it became clear that Sevastopol was to be the next in line. It also became apparent that a land assault would be required since the Allied navy was physically unable to get close enough to the fortress to seriously damage its bastions without the Russians setting fire to its ships by virtue of their relatively accurate guns.[26]

Assault on and Commencement of the Siege of Sevastopol

The initial assault on Sevastopol took place on 17 October 1854 and raged over two days. The location had been chosen for military reasons, since its fortress was the largest of all the Russian naval bases on the Black Sea littoral. Its population of 40,000 was also substantial, 18,000 of whom were military. As such, its military capture was deemed essential for control of Crimea, even if its capital was elsewhere, at Simferopol, 80 kilometres to the northwest.[27]

The fact that Sevastopol consisted of two distinct parts separated by water – in this case the harbour – meant that the encirclement of both was the ideal scenario, since the administrative, mercantile and residential sections were laid out in a splendid Greek neoclassical style to the north, whilst the naval base and its ancillary services were to the south.

To achieve this the Allies marched from the sea around the city, penetrating the forests of the Inkerman Heights towering above the fortress until they established themselves at Mackenzie's Farm, so named because of the eighteenth century Scottish settler who had established it. The siege then commenced. However, the citadel proved to be no easy prey and the siege of Sevastopol continued for eleven and a half months, until September 1855. Moreover, it required a vast expenditure of material and labour, including some 140 million gunshots and 5 million bombs and other shells. No less than 120 kilometres of trenches were dug.[28] It, thus became the longest and most costly siege ever waged in the world until that time.[29]

And it was fiercely waged. On the Russian side, the religious dimension was played on to the full. Indeed, on the eve of the battle, pulpits in the town rang with admonitions that the Allies were supported by the Devil, citing the destruction of St Vladimir's Church.[30] Altogether, 127,583 Russian military personnel were killed at the Battle of Sevastopol and when the Russians finally fled the city, its loss sealed the eventual fate of Russia in the Crimean War, even if that was still some time off.[31]

The Battle of Balaclava and the Charge of the Light Brigade

Meanwhile, the Battle of Balaclava broke out on 25 October 1854. This old port (its name is said to signify a beautiful harbour) had been built by the Genoese and had thrived as a mercantile hub until their expulsion by the Ottomans in the 1400s. The most famous event of this battle is, of course, the charge of the Light Brigade, brought to the world's attention by Alfred Lord Tennyson's poem, published two months after it took place:

> 'Forward, the Light Brigade!'
> Was there a man dismay'd
> Not tho' the soldiers knew
> Someone had blundered:
> Their's not to make reply,
> Their's not to reason why,
> Their's but to do and die:
> Into the valley of Death
> Rode the Six Hundred.

These are inspiring words but the reality was slightly more prosaic, if still deadly: the opposing sides were more evenly matched than was implied in the poem. 661 men had charged, of whom 113 were killed, 134 wounded, and 45 taken prisoner. The Russians suffered proportionally only slightly fewer casualties, with 180 either killed or wounded, out of a total of about 800.[32] The Russians, therefore, felt entitled to see their role in the Battle of Balaklava as an honourable victory, rather than a one-sided slaughter. That said, it brought about no significant gains with respect to the outcome of the war.

The Battle of Inkerman

Of far greater import was the Battle of Inkerman, which took place on 5 November 1854. It was the bloodiest confrontation of the war and, in terms of casualties, almost rivalled those of the Battle of the Somme during the First World War, despite the fact that it lasted only four hours. Casualties amongst the Russians numbered some 12,000, with 2,610 British and 1,726 French also losing their lives.[33] It took days to clear the battlefield of casualties and even as late as twelve days afterwards, four wounded Russian soldiers were found still alive at the bottom of the Quarry Ravine, by the Frenchman and 2nd Zoave Reg. Col. Jean Cler.[34]

The landing of these French forces took place near to the Church of St Vladimir, at Chersonesus, where it was said St Vladimir had first received Orthodox Christianity. It is one of those symbolic ironies of history that this sacred shrine was only a few metres from the place where the French forces landed and set up their camp. Yet such Christian aspects failed to temper the horrors of war. Generals Lord Raglan and de Canrobert complained to Menshikov on 7 November, about the atrocities committed against the Allies, only to be told that their destruction of the Church of St Vladimir at Chersonesus had provoked them.[35] The Allies won, but the victory itself proved to be pyrrhic.

Decline and Death of Tsar Nicholas I and Ascension to the Throne of Alexander II

Throughout the Crimean War, Tsar Nicholas I, supreme autocrat of Russia, was plagued by fears of an Austrian assault on his western flank. Long gone were the days of his grandmother Catherine the Great who had often worked in concert with the Hapsburg emperors, not least in the gobbling up of Poland. For now it was precisely from Austria that he feared that Russian Poland's vulnerability was most threatened. In consequence, he felt himself unable to transfer more troops from Poland to Crimea, however sorely needed they were there. In this restraint he was ardently supported by one of his leading military commanders General Ivan Paskevich, who had been a Russian hero at Inkerman. For if Russian Poland were to be successfully taken over by Austria, the rest of the Russian Empire itself could be expected to collapse in its wake. Sweden seemed to him to be biding its time until the occasion was ripe to retake Finland and other previously Swedish Baltic territories, whilst Britain would be delighted to keep the port of St Petersburg and its protective fortress of Kronstadt permanently bottled up. All this took its toll upon the spirit and body of the Russian emperor. Undermined by influenza-like symptoms which continually worsened and which he, in a state of depression, did nothing to relieve, he summoned the Tsarevitch to what had become his deathbed.

There he humbly confided to his son and heir that, with respect to the soldiers of Crimea, in general, and Sevastopol in particular:

> I have always tried to do my best for them, and, where I failed, it was not for lack of good will, but from the lack of knowledge and intelligence. I ask them to forgive me.[36]

He died on 2 March 1855 from pneumonia and was immediately succeeded by his eldest son, the most liberal of all Russia's imperial princes, who ascended the throne as Alexander II. Now he had to contend with how to resolve the Crimean War.

Only a short time before, in February 1855, the Russians had attacked Yevpatoria which had been defended, with great struggle, by the Ottoman Turks. The following month British troops arrived to reinforce them, but not before the civilian population, in particular, some 40,000 Tatars who had sought refuge from their rural villages, underwent gruelling hardships.[37]

This became integrated into a series of allied pincer movements when to the west of Crimea, their ships attacked and devastated the Russian cities of Mariupol and Taganrog, on the northern coast of the Sea of Azov, north-east of Crimea. The latter's cathedral was badly damaged, its dome destroyed. Those residents who were able to do so fled the city, amongst them, Yevgenia Chekhova, mother of Anton Chekhov the Russian playwright. He was born four years after the war in a house which is now a museum dedicated to his memory.[38]

In Crimea itself, Kerch and Yenikale were now laid waste. This was not so much because of Allied trepidations but a consequence of the fury of Tatars who had many more grievances against the Russian (then as now). Massacre, rape and pillage there anticipated similar depredations in the wars which befell Crimea during the first half of the twentieth century. Even its splendid archaeological museum fell victim to the ravages of war. In *The Times*, William Howard Russell reported:

> The floor of the museum is covered in depth with the debris of broken glass, of vases, urns, statuary, the precious dust of this contents, and charred bits of wood and bone, mingled with the fresh splinters of the shelves, desks, and cases in which they had been preserved. Not a single bit of anything that could be broken or burnt any smaller had been exempt from reduction by hammer and fire.[39]

This was not Britain's finest moment. On the contrary, it rapidly came to light that some British soldiers were involved, officers as well as enlisted men, in pillage and some atrocities committed against the local population. British disciplinary action was summary and strict. Some of the culprits were shot by the twenty British cavalrymen brought in to restore order. Again, *The Times* shed light into this dark moment of the war, quoting a resident of Kerch, with respect to the pillaging, who 'saw several English officers carrying to their ship furniture and sculptures, and all sorts of other items they had plundered from our homes'.[40]

This was not the only occasion when British forces behaved in an unbecoming way. Indeed, no less than 5,546 men, that is about one eighth of all service men were court-martialled for drunkenness alone during the duration of the war.[41] The usual punishment meted out was fifty lashes of the whip and sometimes the docking of a month's pay.

Sharpening of Propaganda against Russia

Back in Britain, at this time, the propaganda against Russia was sharpening. Florence Nightingale's brother-in-law (he was married to her sister Parthenope), Sir Harry Verney, Liberal MP for Buckingham, produced a pamphlet, *Our Quarrel with Russia*, in spring 1855, that was popular and highly influential in government and military circles. In it he tendentiously wrote in words which are still used by those rabidly hostile to Russia to this day:

> Russia is a country which makes no advances in any intellectual or industrial pursuits, and wholly omits to render her influence beneficial to the world. The government from the highest to the lowest is thoroughly corrupt. It lives on the intrigues of agents and on the reports of highly paid spies at home and abroad. It advances into countries more civilised and better governed than its own, and strives to reduce them to its own level of debasement.[42]

Piedmont-Sardinia Joins the Allies

Other European states were now also joining the kill. Piedmont-Sardinia, soon to become the core of a united Italy, entered the fray by accord on 26 January 1855. However, it was only on 8 May, that some 15,000 troops, commanded by General Alfonso La Marmara, arrived in Crimea. Theirs was a welcome contribution to the allied effort and proved an efficient and effective support.

Polish Volunteers and the Goal of an Independent Poland

More worrying to Russia than the Piedmontese and Sardinians though was the role of the Polish Volunteers, whose goals were not merely victory for the Allies in Crimea but an independent Poland. These were largely Polish aristocrats, for the notion of the peasants of Poland also being an integral part of the Polish nation was only just entering their consciousness. In particular, it was Prince Adam Czartoryski who played the greatest role, with his so-called Hôtel Lambert group, a Polish legion of some 1,500 soldiers which received financial support from the Allies. They fought under the banner of the Ottoman sultan, their regimental name, The Sultan's Cossacks, not only in Crimea but also the Caucasus. To Russia, they were clearly traitors, having fled the tsarist army or their private estates in Russian Poland, to join the enemy. They included not only Colonel Kuczynski, the Egyptian army's chief of staff at Yevpatoria, Major Kleczynski and Major Jerzmanowski, but those who took Ottoman names such as Iskander Bey (later Iskander Pasha) and Sadyk Pasha (alias Micha Czaykowski).

Other troops who supported the Allied cause included foreign mercenaries, amongst the most numerous approximately 9,300 Germans, who were also joined by three thousand Swiss. They were first sent to Aldershot, in Hampshire, for training, before they were shipped out to Scutari in November 1855, the first assembly point before their planned transport to Crimea. The war ended, however, before their arrival.[43]

Allied Bluster versus Unpreparedness

Increasing Allied success in Crimea happened despite a dearth of knowledge about it. In western Europe, knowledge of Crimea, even amongst the political and military classes (then as now) was extremely limited. This hampered almost all military engagements. Not only did the allied commanders not have the relevant up-to-date maps, but a basic knowledge of the climate was also absent. Major-General Alexander Macintosh's

Journal of the Crimea, from 1835, contained the misinformation that the peninsula's winter climate was extremely mild and unfortunately the more accurate and recent publication, *The Russian Shoes of the Black Sea in the Autumn of 1852* (1853) by Laurence Oliphant, did not attract the same attention. Therefore, unaware of the winter rigours of Crimea, suitable clothing was unavailable for the campaign. Furthermore – just as in the First World War – most Allied politicians and military personnel suffered from the delusion that the war would be swift, the victory rapidly attained. This was a gross miscalculation which would lead to the deaths of hundreds of thousands.[44]

The French, wary of the Russian climate since their sufferings under Napoleon, were the best equipped of the Allied troops, having sheepskins and special winter coats known as *criméenes*. This created resentment amongst the Allies, as did the cultural differences which distinguished them on all levels. Captain Nigel Kingscote, an aide-de-camp and nephew to Raglan put it succinctly, 'I hate the French' and went on further to complain of French foppishness, in particular, in those surrounding the French commander-in-chief, lamenting that 'All Saint-Arnaud's staff, with one or two exceptions, are just like monkeys, girthed up as tight as they can be and sticking out above and below like balloons.'[45]

British enlisted men were largely appallingly supplied. Their officer class, by contrast, was more favoured for they could always purchase such items on the spot in the thriving markets which flourished there. As Lieutenant Charles Gordon (later to go down in history as Chinese Gordon because of his military prowess in China) wrote to a sister: 'As far as I am concerned, I assure you my dear – I could not be more comfortable in England.'[46] Indeed, Count Vitzthum von Eckstadt, Saxon Minister to London, noted sardonically after the war: 'Several English officers, who went through that rigorous winter, have since told me with a smile that they first learned of the [army's] suffering from the newspapers.'[47]

Nonetheless, back at home, both the monarch, the government and the public did take a keen interest in the well-being of the troops, albeit from their armchairs, once they were aware of the difficulties. The Royal Patriotic Fund was an important means for the provision of succour not only for the soldiers but their families too. Along with money, food and clothing, much of it knitted by hand (including the woollen head covers, with holes for the eyes, nose and mouth, known ever since as balaklavas) were provided by all segments of society. Queen Victoria herself, by no means enthusiastic about the war, wrote to the Duke of Cambridge from Windsor Castle, stating that 'the whole female part' of it, herself included, were 'busily knitting for the army'.[48]

Coping with the Wounded and Sick

Illness amongst all the forces was a major problem even before the war had begun, cooped up as they were on ships with poor hygiene, but even on land the situation was soon dreadful. On the Russian side, after the outbreak of war, the Naryshkin Mansion was given over for use as a hospital for Russian officers by Vorontsov. Amongst the Russian enlisted men, care was more rudimentary. One Russian woman, however, has been singled out by posterity for the succour she provided for them. She was Daria Mikhailova, an eighteen-year-old who was devoted to the memory of her father, a Russian sailor who had lost his life at the Battle of Sinope, when Russian forces had attacked the Ottoman fleet in this northern Anatolian port at the start of the conflict. A symbol of patriotic feminine fervour, she was awarded the Gold Medal for Zeal by Tsar Nicholas I himself in December 1854. This extraordinary honour had otherwise only been given to Russian ladies of noble status. Nicholas's consort, the Alexandra Feodorovna, also awarded her a silver cross simply inscribed with 'Sevastopol', a name by then so pregnant with meaning for all the troops involved.[49] Following Daria Mikhailova's example, some 160 volunteer nurses, many from noble backgrounds, went on to cater for the needs of the Russian military: enlisted men as well as officers. In this respect, it was the Grand Duchess Elena Pavlovna (née Princess Charlotte of Württemberg), consort to the Grand-duke Michael and sister-in-law to the tsar, who was particularly notable. The Community of the Holy Cross which she established after the Battle of Inkerman, became very active in Crimea in this role, welcoming some thirty-four Russian nurses from the higher classes who arrived in Simferopol on a freezing 1 December, after a tiring overland journey from St Petersburg. Many of these soon themselves fell victim to the typhus which raged amongst the debilitated troops. They were supplemented in January in Sevastopol by two further teams of nurses, one of which was personally accompanied by their superintendent Ekaterina Bakunina. Daughter of the governor of St Petersburg and a cousin of the revolutionary anarchist Mikhail Bakunin (then languishing in the Peter and Paul Fortress), she was typical of those dutiful Russian ladies of the highest standing who devoted themselves to service.[50]

The scale of the misery of the wounded and ill amongst the Allied soldiers in Crimea was equally great with more suffering from disease than from military action during the war. With respect to them, the role of the British nurse Florence Nightingale (1820–1910) became a global legend, her devotion and commitment to her military charges, commemorated, amongst others, by a monumental statue at Waterloo Place, in London, erected by the sculptor Arthur George Walker in 1914. It was eventually joined by that of Secretary of War Sidney Herbert (made in 1866 by J.H. Foley R.A.), who had provided her with the political support needed for her activities.

Nightingale's background was by no means extraordinary for a girl of her milieu and gave no indication of the role she would play. Yet the fact that her father was a highly prosperous industrialist of religious beliefs in Derbyshire and that a strong Anglican Christian code of ethics informed her attitude to life doubtless played a role in forming her strong independent personality and propelling it in the service of others in need. Unusually, for a girl of her background, she had spent time at a Lutheran religious community at Kaiserswerth-am-Rhein in the vicinity of Düsseldorf in the German Rhineland. There she encountered Pastor Theodor Fliedner, who, with his deaconesses, devoted themselves to caring for the sick. It was their model of nursing which she took back with her to Britain when she returned home in 1851. So when the public at home became aware that no provision had been made for nurses to care for the wounded and ill in the war, she took matters into her own hands. The greatest difficulty with respect to the Crimean War itself in regard to the wounded and ill was not so much on the battlefields themselves, but 500 kilometres away at the Allied hospital at Scutari, in Constantinople, to which the injured and ill were removed by steamship.

By 12 October 1854 it had become clear in Britain – for the steamship also meant that news travelled quickly – that, as *The Times* correspondent in Constantinople, Thomas Chenery, put it, 'no sufficient medical preparations have been made for the proper care of the wounded'. As a result, the '*Times*

Crimean Fund for the Relief of the Sick and Wounded' was established by Sir Robert Peel, whose father had formerly been prime minister.[51] The Secretary at War, Herbert, then appointed Nightingale to the post of Superintendent of the Female Nursing Establishment of the English General Hospitals in Turkey, to which the injured were brought by ship. The first team of thirty-eight nurses, with Nightingale, reached Scutari on 4 November 1854, just after the Battle of Balaklava.

The laying of the telegraph to the western Black Sea port of Varna (then Ottoman but now in Bulgaria), made communications almost instantaneous. Henceforth, the public were almost immediately aware of the needs of the troops. Nurses poured into Scutari over the following year and half and in the spring of 1856, Nightingale's remit was extended to Crimea itself. As a result of her close personal connection to Herbert and his wife and the regular communication between them, endless channels of bureaucracy were avoided. Moreover, in contrast to the Russians, amongst whom professional nurses were recruited largely from young women of the working classes (but also some Roman Catholic nuns) largely because they were thought more inured to difficult working conditions and used to being bossed around, the British nurses were largely middle class.[52]

The second team arrived at Christmas time and were well equipped with medicines and the other materials needed for the care of the patients. However, no amount of political clout in London, nor funds provided by the Times Crimean Fund were able to deal with the vast problems of hygiene faced by the hospital at Scutari. Not only was understanding of the spread of infection and poor hygiene little understood, but the hospital itself, formerly a military barracks, was built over cesspits. In February 1855, the mortality rate there was 52 per cent, 8 per cent higher than when Nightingale had first arrived, and of whom only a small minority had actually been injured on the battlefield. Indeed, by the time spring arrived, some four thousand soldiers had succumbed to epidemic illnesses and other infections.[53] In Crimea, matters had improved slightly, since hospitals, however primitive, had been set up for the Allies, at Inkerman, on the Mackenzie Height, as well as in the Palace of the Khans at Bakhchisaray itself.

Medical Innovations

However, as with the Second World War's, introduction of penicillin on a global scale to combat infection, so the Russian wars in the Caucasus, in the 1840s, also produced medical innovations, eventually useful in Crimea. One individual of immense stature in their introduction was Nikolai Pirogov (1810–1881). A native of Moscow, he had commenced his medical studies at Moscow University at the age of fourteen, later becoming professor in medicine at the University of Dorpat (today Tartu, in Estonia, but then a part of Russia), and, thereafter, Professor of Surgery at the Academy of Military Medicine in St Petersburg. Sent, in 1847, with the Russian army to the Caucasus to quell tribal uprisings, he introduced the use of ether as an anaesthetic in dealing with war injuries and amputations. This innovation, together with other new procedural implementations, proved of immense value for Russian forces in the Crimean War. Whereas the Russians were now able to accomplish more than a hundred amputations, on three tables, in a seven hour stretch, the Allies were still following old fashioned and, by comparison, inefficient procedures. In part, this was because of an ideology which saw the use of ether as debilitating in the longer term recovery of the patient, in part because it required what was deemed too much expertise to administer. Far more Russians therefore survived amputations than their enemy counterparts. Of course, what also mattered was that Pirogov had turned his attentions to other medical improvements with respect to hospital care. At the bombardment of Sevastopol, for example, he introduced the use of triage. According to this practice, wounded men were sorted into three groupings before they were accommodated, much less even treated. Priority was given to those seriously injured but only those with a good prognosis of recovery. Next those with lesser injuries were treated. Finally, those whose chances for survival were deemed very poor were given only remedial comfort and care, rather than treated for recovery, in essence, like that provided in a modern hospice for the dying today.

A fascinating insight into this arrangement was left by Leo Tolstoy who visited the Great Hall at Sevastopol into which those considered treatable were removed (the terminally wounded were taken to barracks to die). In 'Sevastopol in December', he observed:

No sooner have you opened the door than you are assailed without warning by the sight and smell of about forty or fifty amputees and critically wounded, some of them on camp beds, but most of them lying on the floor.... you will see fearsome sights that will shake you to the roots of your being; you will see war not as a beautiful, orderly, and gleaming formation, with music and beaten drums, streaming banners and generals on prancing horses, but war in its authentic expression – as blood, suffering and death.[54]

Poor Nutrition

For many of the enlisted men – but not the officers – serving in the various military forces, except for the French, the lack of nutrition was a major problem. This was especially true amongst the Ottoman forces. Out of some 4,000 Turkish soldiers who fought at Balaklava on 25 October 1854, half would eventually die from malnutrition by the end of that year. Untold others were not fit for action even before the engagement for that very reason.[55]

French troops, by contrast, enjoyed an enviable infrastructure, which included cooks and at least one baker for each regiment. There were also numerous sutlers, that is, the *vivandières* and *cantinières*, uniformed women serving from field canteens. Of particular significance amongst the French was the circumstance that food in general was collectively served, as opposed to the situation in the British camp, where rations were cooked by the men individually. The greater efficiency, hygiene and nutritional value of the French system became so obvious that it was eventually introduced amongst the British as well but not before there was much malnutrition and loss of life.[56] Indeed, in mid-December 1854, there was a virtual total absence of fruit and vegetables for British enlisted men, with lemon and lime juice providing the only means of avoiding scurvy (the popular custom, especially in the United States, of adding them to tea remains with us to the present). Officers, on the other hand, frequently purchased a plethora of luxury comestibles, including hams and cheeses, chocolates and cigars, even wine and champagne, sometimes sent in hampers by Fortnum & Mason of London to the local shops of Balaklava and Kadikoi.

Mary Seacole

It was against this background, that the Jamaican shopkeeper Mary Seacole (1805–81) arrived in Crimea. A highly enterprising widow (her portrait painted by the British artist Albert Charles Challen in 1869 can be viewed in the National Portrait Gallery, London), her so-called 'British hotel', was, in reality, at least in her words, 'a mess-table and comfortable quarters for sick and convalescent officers'. For that reason she was posthumously awarded the Jamaican Order of Merit in 1991. However, controversy as to the degree in which altruism, rather than commercial acumen, played a role in her Crimean activities, has not yet been resolved. In any case, for the thousands of Allied ill and wounded enlisted men who had few resources the outlook was bleak. For them, poor nutrition, on the one hand, and bad hygiene on the other, took a horrendous toll. In consequence, by January 1855, active British military forces numbered 11,000, fewer than half of those available in November 1854.[57]

Conclusion of the Siege of Sevastapol

The siege of Sevastapol which had begun quite early in the war still dragged on and on. This was in part because of its defensive system of trenches and earth works, constructed by the highly able Imperial Russian general and engineer Eduard Totleben (1818–84, he was of Baltic German origins) and to whom a great monument would be constructed at Sevastopol in 1909. In some respects, this siege anticipated the battles of attrition in the First World War. Moreover, as in that conflagration, occasionally, some fraternisation might occur between the opposing forces. One such event was witnessed by British Captain Nathaniel Steevens, 88th Regiment of Foot (Connaught Rangers):

> Here we saw a crowd of English officers and Men mingled with some Russian Officers & escort, who had brought out the Flag of Truce; this was the most curious sight of all; the Officers chatted together as freely and gaily as if the warmest friends, and as for the Soldiers, those who 3 minutes before had been firing away at each other, might now be seen smoking together, sharing tobacco and drinking Rum, exchanging the usual compliments of 'bono Ingles'; the Russian Officers were very gentlemanly looking men, spoke French and one English; at length on reference to watches it was found 'time was nearly up' so

both parties gradually receded from each others' sight to their respective works, not hover without our men shaking hands with the Russian soldiers and some one calling out, 'Au revoir.'[58]

Such occasions, however, were rare exceptions. The reality of the siege for most of the time was one of unrelenting bombardment. Indeed, 500 British and French artillery pieces fired unceasingly, almost doubling their fire power compared to the commencement in October. As such, it was the most powerful assault of its kind ever waged. Nor were civilian targets spared: the entire city of Sevastopol was a target, from hospitals and schools to military barracks. Women and children, as well as soldiers, fell victim to the fiery onslaught, which evoked no international public outcry as it would do today.[59]

Lord Raglan's decision to keep the army encamped on the Heights created a furore within the High Command – both Evans and Cambridge returned to Britain in a rage, followed in their wake by many other officers, some 225 of the total of 1,540 officers. Only 60 of the former returned. In the meantime, the death rate amongst the enlisted men was appalling.[60] Even grandees like the Duke of Cambridge, out in Crimea at the time, felt the war taking its toll on their health. A letter to his personal doctor says it all:

I hope you will not object to my going for a short time to Constantinople, Gibson [his doctor] being of opinion that if I were at this moment to return to Camp in this dreadful weather I should only have to take to my bed.[61]

Various futile Allied assaults were carried out on the Malakhov and the Redan, but for ages these seemed to achieve nothing. The Russian offensive to take the Traktir Bridge under General Liprandi, with no less than 47,000 infantrymen and 10,000 cavalry, supported by 270 field guns, faced the Sardinians. Other Russian forces under General Read, a Russian whose Scottish father had immigrated because of the opportunities for engineers, faced the French. He was soon killed by a shell, Prince Mikhail Dmitrievich Gorchakov (1793–1861) thereupon succeeding him in command. By now, though, morale in Sevastopol, especially after Vice-Admiral Nakhimov's death, was finally beginning to collapse. Some 2,273 soldiers had lost their lives on the Chernaia river, not to mention almost 4,000 wounded casualties. 1,742 Russian soldiers went missing, the majority thought to be deserters. Even General Osten-Sacken began to expect the worse and plans to evacuate were finally set in motion.[62] The Russians gave way and the Malakhov Tower was finally taken by the French under General Patrice de MacMahon (later Duke of Magenta) on 8 September 1855.

The sights which awaited the Allies on entering Sevastopol were harrowing. Russell, who was there, went on to write in *The Times*:

> Of all the pictures of the horrors of war which have ever been presented to the world, the hospital of Sevastopol offered the most heartrending and revolting. Entering one of these doors, I beheld such a sight as few men, thank God, have ever witnessed: ... the rotten and festering corpses of the soldiers, who were left to die in their extreme agony, untended, uncared for, packed as close as they could be stowed... saturate with blood which oozed and trickled through upon the floor, fuming with the droppings of corruption.[63]

Baron Bondurand, the French military intendant, to Marshal de Castellane, gave his own impressions. On 21 September 1855, he noted:

> The town is literally crushed to bits. There is not a single house that our projectiles missed. There are no roofs left at all, and almost all the walls have been destroyed. The garrison must have taken huge casualties in this siege where all our blows counted. It is a testimony to the indisputable spirit and endurance of the Russians, who held on for so long and only surrendered when their position became untenable with our capture of the Malakhov.[64]

As the new tsar Alexander II put it, on 14 September 1855, in a philosophical though, in retrospect, rather upbeat tone and certainly a view not shared today, 'Sevastopol is not Moscow. The Crimea is not Russia'.[65]

It was just as well that was the case, since the ruined city soon became a major focus of 'military tourism'. Ship after ship of British and Continental tourists arrived to comb over the battlefields, returning home with souvenirs, some bought, others filched, making many armchair soldiers feel as if they too had contributed to the victory.

1856 – End of the War

In the spring of 1856, the Crimean War finally drew to a close with the defeat of Russia. The Paris Peace Conference had little to resolve, since matters had long since been agreed in congress by the Allies, and so took only three sessions to conclude the final settlement, the Treaty of Paris, signed at 1pm, on 30 March that year. A plethora of grand festivities were held in this Europe's most splendid capital, not least that which celebrated the birth of an heir and only child to the Emperor Napoleon III and his consort the Empress Eugénie. This was the Prince Imperial, Louis Napoleon, who would die young, unmarried and without issue in exile during the Anglo-Zulu War, fought in what is now South Africa, in 1879. Despite the telegraph, it would take until 2 April for all the guns of the Crimean War to fall silent. A further six months were required for the Allied evacuation to be effected. Before departing, though, the British made sure that the Sevastopol docks were in ruins and the French that Fort Nicholas was no more.

Final Toll of the Crimean War

When the final toll is taken, the human costs of the Crimean War were enormous. Over 750,000 men lost their lives, a figure comparable to that of the American Civil War of 1861–65 which was soon to follow. Most of these died not in battle nor of wounds but from epidemic illnesses. Russia alone accounted for half a million dead, with the French losing some 100,000 (out of a total of 310,000 personnel), the British 20,813 (out of a total of about 98,000 personnel, four fifths from illness rather than battle).[66]

With respect to the British forces, surprisingly, although the backdrop of the Irish famine only a few years before makes it more comprehensible, it was, disproportionately, the Irish troops who fought, as well as gave up their lives amongst enlisted men. Startling, for example, that just under one third of the males normally residing at Whitegate, Aghada and Farsid in County Cork died in the Crimean War.[67]

The Allied victory notwithstanding, the results of the war were ultimately inconclusive. Although southern parts of Bessarabia, seized in 1812, had to be returned by Russia to the Ottomans and the Black Sea itself was demilitarised, the principal damage to the tsarist government was the loss of prestige and influence of Nicholas I himself and the old imperial order which he had seemed to embody. Thus, his successor, Alexander II felt compelled to undertake a thorough modernisation not only of the military, but of the empire itself.

It was the Tatars who suffered the most in Crimea, both during and in the wake of the war, and the overwhelming majority of them emigrated in a great diaspora – more than 141,000, leaving no more than 103,000 in Crimea. Their place was taken by an influx of other Christians, who became the Crimean majority population – not only Russian, Ukrainian and various ethnic minorities of the Russian Empire, but Germans and Greeks, as well. That said, many Tatars who remained did find a satisfactory accommodation with the Russian state. Indeed, by the middle of the nineteenth century, the ulema of Crimea had become a privileged estate of its own, whose spiritual offices were passed from father to son.

Entrepreneurial individuals from Britain also tried to exploit new economic opportunities in the region, in particular, such British industrialists and businessmen as Sir Culling Eardly and Moses Montefiore, who secured the purchase of the Balaklava Railway, not for redevelopment in Crimea but for transfer to Ottoman Palestine where the railway material, it was hoped, could be used for the construction of a railway from Jaffa, on the Mediterranean coast, to Jerusalem. This proved too visionary for the time and in the end the railway material was sold off for scrap.

As for Russia, it learnt important lessons for the future, in particular, the need to abolish serfdom and to establish a body of conscripted men of a higher educational standard than serf troops could provide, as well as the need for a vastly improved transport infrastructure. Britain, too, learnt much from the war. After Lord Edward Cardwell became Minister for War under Prime Minister William Gladstone, he introduced a series of reforms, which eschewed the old practice of purchasing commissions, in favour of promotions earned through merit. Conditions for the soldiers were improved, including shorter periods of enlistment, abolishment of peacetime flogging and a dispersion of command into the wider middle classes. For, as the American author Nathaniel Hawthorne, known for his frontier novel *Last of the Mohicans*, wrote in his *English Notebooks*, the military action of 1854 had 'done the work of fifty ordinary ones' in discrediting the military leadership of the aristocracy amongst all the warring parties.[68] Yet there was no doubt that the war had produced heroes among all involved, aristocracy, yeomen and enlisted men. In Britain, the Victoria Cross was established as the highest honour awarded to such individuals and no less than sixty-two veterans of the war received it, including sixteen privates, four gunners and a sapper, from the army, and two seamen and three boatswains, from the navy.[69] Thus, for both Russia and the Allies, the Crimean War led to the creation of a modern military, in which the latest technology and improved education for the masses played an increasingly major role.

THE AFTERMATH OF THE CRIMEAN WAR

The Ottoman Empire after the War: Its Expectations Unfulfilled

The Allied victory in the Crimean War did not bring many of the benefits that had been expected. The Sultan, Abdülmeçid, with his courtiers, and some members of the Allied governments had hoped that Crimea would be ceded by Russia to the Ottomans. This, however, did not transpire and, indeed, other members of the Allies were not particularly concerned by the fact. However, they did expect some gains from the Sultan and his government for at least trying, namely the granting of religious toleration towards Christians living under his turban. When the Sultan unexpectedly accepted invitations to attend two ambassadorial balls in February in Constantinople, organised by the British, and French respectively, the successful granting of religious toleration for the empire's Christians seemed likely. As guest of honour at these events, the attire of the sultan and his multi-religious court became the focus of diplomatic chatter. As Lady Emelia Hornby who attended the British costume ball noted on the following day:

> It would take me a day to enumerate half the costumes. But everyone who had been to Queen's balls costumés agreed that they did not approach this one in magnificence; for besides the gathering of French, Sardinian and English officers, the people of the country appeared in their own superb and varied costumes; and the groups were beyond all description beautiful. The Greek Patriarch, the Armenian Archbishop, the Jewish High Priest were there in their robes of state. ...Abdülmeçid quietly walked up the ballroom with Lord and Lady Stratford, their daughters, and a gorgeous array of Pashas in the rear.[1]

The French had capped the British in showing their appreciation to the Sultan, by having their ambassador, Édouard-Antoine de Thouvenel, award him the Medal of the Légion d'Honneur. This he proudly wore to their ball. Moreover, the sultan's wives, as well as other high born ladies of the court also attended, overcoming their centuries old retirement from male company. Henceforth, they engaged in festive and other social events increasingly like their European sisters. Eschewing traditional Ottoman robes, they attired themselves in the manner of European aristocratic ladies, even to the degree of using corsets.

Yet outside the rarified circles of court life, little seemed to have changed in the empire and converts who abandoned Islam for Christianity continued to suffer the death penalty, the Sultan's promises notwithstanding. Lord Stratford wrote to the Porte on 23 December 1856:

> The great European powers can never consent to perpetuate by the triumphs of their fleets and armies the enforcement in Turkey of a law {apostasy}, which is not only a standing insult to them, but a source of cruel persecution to their fellow Christians. They are entitled to demand, the British Government distinctly demands, that the Mohammedan who turns Christian shall be as free from every kind of punishment on that account as the Christian who embraces the Mohammedan faith.[2]

This matter would ultimately be taken up by another Ottoman royal, Prince Moustapha Fazil, the grandson of Muhammad Ali Pasha of Egypt, whose descendants ruled the country until King Farouk's overthrow in 1952. In a well-publicised letter to Sultan Abdul Aziz in 1866, he endeavoured to bring home the need for the Ottoman government to modernise, adopt religious toleration and make all its subjects equal before the law with the right to freedom of expression. He was successful in getting the support of the sultan who had visited Britain in 1867.[3] However, more conservative elements resisted and focused their wrath leading to the deposition of Abdul Aziz in 1876. Shortly thereafter it was officially recorded that he had committed suicide by cutting his wrists with scissors. He was succeeded by Murad V, who was himself deposed after only ninety- three days, ostensibly because of similar inclinations to institute liberal reforms. Islamic tradition with respect to other religions had triumphed.

Ottoman Victory over Russia Proves Pyrrhic

Despite Russia's defeat in the Crimean War, over the longer term the aggrandisement of its political influence and allies at the cost of the Ottoman Empire continued. Indeed, Russia renewed and strengthened its support for the other Slavic nations striving for the removal of the 'Ottoman yoke'. When, in 1862, the Turks bombarded Belgrade, Russia came to their defence, calling for a reconvocation of those who had signed the Treaty of Paris after the Crimean War. This took place at Kanlidze, by Constantinople, and led to the final evacuation of Ottoman troops from Serbia in 1867. With Serbian official independence now secured, Russian prestige was rising and the creation of a Balkan League was mooted. The Russian fanning of Pan-Slavic flames increased and, in spring 1876, came to a head with Bulgarian uprisings, evoked by the massive immigration to Ottoman Bulgaria of some half a million Tatars and Circassians, many semi-nomadic, who had fled Crimea and the Caucasus, respectively. Many of these Muslim immigrants lost their lives in the ensuing massacres and the Ottomans carried out reprisals against the Christians, employing their notoriously brutal military irregulars, the Bashi Bazouks, drawn from amongst the local population, who massacred some 12,000 Christians. Of particular notoriety was the burning alive of a thousand or so Christians who had taken refuge in the parish church of the village of Batak, in Bulgaria. Only one elderly woman survived to tell the tale.[4] Russian journals, such as those of the *Russian World* (under the proprietorship of its editor-in-chief, General Mikhail G. Cherniaev, former military governor of Turkestan) rushed to their support. When Russian troops then invaded Bulgaria, in January 1878, taking Adrianople (modern-day Erdine) and almost reaching the gates of Constantinople, the Russian Grand-duke Nikolai wrote to his brother, the Grand-duke Constantine that: 'We must go to the centre, to Tsargrad, and there finish the holy cause you have assumed.'[5]

This was not to be, but with the restoration of its Black Sea status completed seven years before, Russia had succeeded in reversing all the territorial losses it had suffered in the aftermath of the Crimean War.

Partial Collapse of the Tatar Community

It was the Tatar community which ultimately suffered the most of all ethnic communities after the conclusion of the Crimean War. Having to a significant degree aided the Allied victors and suffered the greatest privations of all civilians, it might have been expected that the British, French and, in particular, their fellow Muslim Ottoman Turks would have secured major benefits for them at the peace settlement. However, this was not the case. Rather, their presence was largely ignored and they were left to the mercies of the returning Russian authorities who viewed them as a third column which had betrayed the Russian Orthodox people. Some 15,000 Tatars, therefore, fled, along with a further 50,000 Nogai Tatars, many of whom lived just across the Sea of Azov to the northeast of Crimea. Indeed, by 1867, 104,211 Tatar men and 88,149 Tatar women had departed from Crimea, a form of ethnic cleansing in which they had felt compelled to abandon no less than 784 villages and 457 mosques, the former of which were soon occupied by immigrating Christians.[6]

Sometimes, this Tatar flight left the refugees in a worse state than had they remained in Crimea. For example, many had fled to Ottoman Circassia, in the Caucasus, or to the Ottoman Balkan provinces, only to find that Russian conquests of these territories once again made them unwilling subjects of the tsar. Thus, up to 90,000 of these refugee Tatars pulled up stakes once again, fleeing during the late 1870s to the Ottoman heartland of Anatolia.[7]

Modernisation and Re-organisation of the Russian Military

One thing that had become clear to the Russian government, above all, was the need to modernise and reorganise the military. Therefore, in 1857, the Grand Duke Constantine, younger brother to Alexander II, who had himself become an admiral of the Russian fleet, instigated reforms. Like Peter the Great before him, he travelled abroad to acquire expertise, in his case, going first to Paris, where he sought technical collaboration. This rapprochement with France not only sapped the blood out of much of the Treaty of Paris with respect to the Black Sea clauses, but it allowed Russia to pursue a policy of armed neutrality with some 300,000 troops on its western borders with Austria, much as the latter had done during the Crimean War against Russia. This benefited France for it removed the pressure of a surge of new Austrian troops in Italy, obliging them to be stationed instead in Galicia to ward off any possible Russian attack. It was on this basis that the French and Piedmontese began their successful war against Austria in April 1859, which would ultimately lead to the success of the *Risorgimento* and the establishment of a united Italy.

The Grand Duke Constantine then moved on to the Villafranca (today's Villefranche-sur-mer, in France) then under the sovereignty of the Kingdom of Sardinia. Its prime minister Count Camillo Cavour offered him the option of leasing a coaling station for the Russian navy which he accepted. Thus Russia seemed to go from strength to strength, wiping out some of the humiliation caused by the destruction of its fleet and naval docks in the Crimean War. One innovation was the publication of a military handbook by the military reformer Dmitry Miliutin, but more important was the emancipation of the serfs which Tsar Alexander II promulgated on 19 February 1861. This ensured that poorly educated serfs would never again form a part of his modern armies. Henceforth, with the introduction of primary compulsory education throughout the empire, all recruits would have some level of basic knowledge and skills. This was augmented, in 1874, by the introduction of universal conscription for all males regardless of background at the age of twenty, thereby creating the ethos of a 'people's army'. In the meantime, though, the Crimean War had entered the Russian public consciousness as something positive and a Museum of the Black Sea Fleet at Sevastopol was established in 1869, by private subscription. Bodies were never fully recovered from the battle site and even in our own time bones of the fallen have been recovered. Latterly, these were reburied at the Museum of Alma near Bakhchisaray with full military honours and in the presence of both Ukrainian and Russian officials. And now, with the transfer of sovereignty to Russia, a Russian Orthodox chapel of commemoration will also be constructed there.

Resettlement of Anti-Russian Christians

The conclusion of the Crimean War did not only bode ill for many Muslim Tatars who had turned against Russia; Christian enemies of Russian rule who had come from within the Russian Empire to fight on the side of the Allies in the war – such as many Poles – were also forced permanently to leave their homeland and to re-establish themselves elsewhere abroad. Thousands of those who had made up the Polish Legion in Crimea, also known as the Ottoman Cossacks, seeking independence for Russian Poland, were amongst their number and they were warmly received by the Ottoman government. Some were resettled in Ottoman Dobrudja, now the eastern coastal regions of Romania and Bulgaria. Others went to Asian Anatolia, but most famously, some, especially those of high noble background, went to Adampol (Polonezkoi), a suburb of Constantinople which had been founded by Prince Adam Czartoryski, the leader of the Polish emigration, in 1842, and named in his honour.

Orthodox Consolidation

With the retirement in 1855 of Prince Mikhail Semyonovich Vorontsov as governor in New Russia, the old social order seemed to come to an end. In his place arrived Count Sergei Grigoriyevich Stroganov (1794–1882) who infused the civil administration with Nicholas I's ideological triad of 'Orthodoxy, Autocracy and Nationality' as had been propagated by Sergey Uvarov, Russian Minister of Education in 1833, and which found resonance in the writings of such great literary figures as Nikolai Gogol and Fedor Tyutchev. In this he was actively supported by Innokenty, the Archbishop of the Diocese of Kherson-Tauride, in which Crimea lay. To further the missionary activities of the region he encouraged both the establishment of a new Diocese of Crimea itself, and the foundation of several monastic houses.[8]

Archbishop Innokenty also saw the need to fill the vacuum left by departing Tatars with new Christian immigrants who would further the propagation of Russian Orthodoxy. Supporting him, the Russian government promulgated a law in 1862 which granted privileges and subsidies to the new arrivals. These included not only Orthodox adherents such as Russians, Greeks, Armenians, Bulgarians and Bessarabians, but non-Orthodox Christians including Germans and Baltic peoples. This had economic benefits as well, as the Armenians and Greeks were successful merchants and traders who were useful for the return of Sevastopol and

Yevpatoria to prosperity. Whilst the decline of the old khanate strongholds of Kaffa (Feodosia), Gözleve and Bakhchisaray continued, no less than 330 abandoned Tatar villages were repopulated by the new Christian immigrants, with the mosques transformed into churches and new ones constructed. One such is the Resurrection Church overlooking the sea at Foros, built by the Russian architect N. Shagin in 1892, who worked in the National Russian style of which the Church of the Saviour on the Spilled Blood in St Petersburg is the most prominent example. Crimea, thus, had become a radically different place in the final decade of the nineteenth century. When, in 1882, Vorontsov died and the great palace of Alupka passed into other hands, the 'enlightened' religiously cosmopolitan Vorontsov period was definitely at an end. Rather it was now an almost Orientalist view of Russia's destiny which came to the fore, perhaps best expressed by the Russian author and Orthodox believer Fedor Dostoyevsky. For him the Crimean War had been the 'crucifixion of the Russian Christ' and he lyrically expounded:

> Unclear to you is her predestination.
> The East – is hers. To her a million generations
> Untiringly stretch out their hands….
> And the resurrection of the ancient East
> By Russia (so God has commanded) is drawing near.[9]

Yet, for all these difficulties, the Crimean population grew and by 1897, there were some 546,000 people living in Crimea, albeit only 35 per cent of them now Crimean Tatars.[10] An improved transport infrastructure was also improving the region. The railway arrived from St Petersburg and Moscow in 1875, benefiting from the construction of a bridge by Sivash, which terminated at Sevastopol.

The new tsar Alexander II declared Crimea to be the cradle of Russian Christianity and to this end encouraged the rebuilding, restoration and construction of cathedrals, churches and monasteries. Already, in 1861, he had initiated the reconstruction of the great Cathedral of St Vladimir at Chersonesus, a monumental endeavour which would only be finished in 1892. The Cathedral of St Alexander Nevsky, in Simferopol, the construction of which had begun in 1829 was eventually completed in 1881, whilst that of St Vladimir Equal to the Apostles was completed in the years 1858–88. Then in the final years of the century, Crimea's last great spate of church building ensued: the St Alexander Nevsky Cathedral, at Yalta (1892), built by the architect Nikolai Krasnov; the Resurrection Cathedral at Foros (1888–92) by Nikolai Chagin; St Catherine at Feodosia (1892), the Holy Mother of God the Protectress at Sevastopol (1892– 1905) and finally that of St Nicholas the Wonder Worker at Yevpatoria (1893–99).

New Wave of Jewish Immigration to Crimea

In the final two decades of the nineteenth century, a new wave of Jewish immigration also arrived in Crimea. They came from the Pale of Settlement in the west of Russia, annexed in the late eighteenth century from Poland, and Crimea was one of the few regions of empire in which they were not only permitted to settle but actively encouraged to do so. These were Ashekenazic Jews, who in 1881, numbered about 10,000. This was only the first of further waves of Jewish immigration which, in 1897, had grown to more than 24,000. Eighty per cent of them settled in the major cities of Crimea: Sevastopol, Feodosia, Kerch and Simferopol, where they could carry on mercantile activities.[11]

The Karaites as a Privileged Minority

Although the Jews of the Russian Empire were generally a disadvantaged minority, the non-Talmudic Karaites were another matter. Based at Yevpatoria, in the later nineteenth century, where many had moved from Chufut Kale, they were relatively wealthy and exerted an economic influence far beyond their small community of only 5,400 (in 1897).[12] Amongst the most noted figures of the Karaites at that time was Abraham Firkovich (1832–74), writer, archaeologist and collector – actually a native of Lutsk in today's western Ukraine, but then in the Russian Empire – who had moved to Crimea. It was he who brought an awareness of Karaite culture to the wider world.

Tsar Nicholas II as a Humanitarian

In 1894, Tsar Nicholas II ascended the Russian throne and his assumption of autocratic powers seemed to bode well for the maintenance of European peace, especially since he had visited Britain the previous year, and indeed, the United States before that, learning about western liberal values. Rather than focusing upon concepts of electoral representation, however, he sought to mitigate the horrors of war, with respect to the codification of conduct during wars, as advocated by the so-called 'peace movement'. These were only too well remembered by the Russians from the Crimean War, as well as from the later Balkan ones. Numerous international conferences were organised on this theme, two of which took place on the initiative of Nicholas II himself, in 1899 and in 1907, both at The Hague, in the Netherlands. As Fyodor Fyodorovich Martens, the tsar's international lawyer, put it in a declaration adopted by the 1899 conference:

> It is our unanimous desire that the armies of the civilised nations be not simply provided with the most murderous and perfect weapons, but that they shall also be imbued with a notion of right, justice and humanity, binding even in invaded territory and even in regard to the enemy.[13]

The rule of law was thus given a new focus throughout the Russian Empire, including in Crimea. As an aside, it should be noted that in the middle of his reign, in 1905, Crimean judicial records – some 121 volumes – were removed from Simferopol, to the Imperial Library in St Petersburg, the capital from which the centralised Russian state ruled over Crimea, both judicially and politically.[14]

Tatar Reforms

The late nineteenth century was a period of reform not only amongst Russians but also for some of the Muslim Tatar population of the Crimea. One of the principal leaders advocating reform there was Ismail Bey Gaspirali (Gasprinsky, in Russian; 1851–1914). A teacher in Arabic (few Crimean Tatars understood this language) in the upper level classes at the local Islamic theological academy in his native Bakhchisaray, he had gone on to become the governor of Bakhchisaray (1877–81), donning western rather than Tatar attire. He joined the so-called *Jadid* (Modern) movement, popular among many of the Russian Muslim ulema in the 1880s. This sought to revitalise and reform Islam in Crimea by encouraging modernist interpretations of the Qur'an which would enable a greater appreciation of the values of modern science and education amongst the Tatars. To this end, he founded the newspaper *Tercuman* (*Interpreter*, in English; *Perevodchik*, in Russian) in 1883, which was published in Bakhchisaray and continued in print until 1914. His main goal was to further the unity of the Tatars, in particular, but the Turkic peoples, and even the wider Muslim community, more generally. Therefore, his newspaper had articles not only in Russian, but in Ottoman Turkish (which used the Arabic script), but in a more demotic form in which Persian and Arabic vocabulary and other usages were replaced with local Tatar vernacular.

Its influence went far beyond Crimea, and attracted a Turkic readership from throughout the Russian Empire, in particular in Central Asia. Secular schools were also established, the most noted of which was at Bakhchisaray in 1884. Gaspirali was particularly keen to introduced his so-called New Method, which envisioned courses in geography, history and mathematics, taught through the media of both Ottoman Turkish and Russian. The Muslim ulema objected vociferously, not only because they saw the intrusion of secularism but because of the equality of the sexes which Gaspirali's advocation of such secular education for women seemed to encourage. Gaspirali also went on to briefly publish *Public School* (1910), a Russian journal, in Bakrhchisaray, whilst his daughter Shefka Hanim Gaspirali (1886–1975), a leading figure in the Crimean women's movement, edited another short-lived Tatar periodical *Women's World* (1906–07).

Yet Gaspirali was by no means an ultra radical. In fact, he was endeavouring to discourage Tatar emigration to the Ottoman Empire by making the lot of Tatars more palatable at home. He advocated the adoption by all Turkic peoples of a single Turkic language and, whilst exhorting Islamic beliefs and values, he also supported greater rights for women. Mathematics and geography now took their places among the usual religious subjects taught in the traditional madrasa. Their popularity burgeoned and by 1916, there were some 5,000 *Jadid* schools throughout Russia, many of them in Crimea. Often perceived as undermining the

Orthodox character of Mother Russia and as breeding grounds for anti-Russian pan-Turkic political movements, the Russian state increasingly sought to control them, especially after the success of the German-influenced Young Turk movement, which had made the sultan a mere figurehead, in the Ottoman capital during and after the revolution of 1908–09 there, albeit to little avail.

Lower down the social scale, however, the overwhelming majority of Tatars were illiterate, subsisting at just above an existential minimum. They were generally employed as tenant farmers, often on small plots of land in the mountainous interior or on the northern steppes. Others, though, worked as artisans in a wide range of crafts. As elsewhere in the rural regions of the Russian Empire they had come to be administered in each community since the 1870s by the *zemtsvo*, a communal unit of local government instituted by the relatively liberal Alexander II. Endowing these bodies with money, primary schools, clinics and other such foundations were established for their benefit. However, corruption was rife and, in reality, however well-meaning the initiative was, the development of this infrastructure was limited. Indeed, as the century drew to a close, even in the capital, Simferopol, there was only one doctor on call for some 14,000 inhabitants, whilst in Yalta, by then Crimea's most prosperous resort town, only 7,000 residents depended upon his services.[15] The degree of medical care in the often remote rural and mountainous areas in which many Tatars lived can therefore be imagined.

Growing Tatar Political Radicalism

During the early years of the twentieth century, many Tatars became increasingly politically radicalised. Some resided in Constantinople, where Noman Chelebi-Jihan and Jafer Seydamet agitated through first the Student Association (1908) and later the underground Fatherland Society (1909), which stirred up a more extreme form of Crimean Tatar nationalism. Many of their supporters were Crimean Tatars living outside Crimea in other parts of the Ottoman Empire, particularly the Balkans. The poet and primary school teacher Shevki Bektöre, was one such, a native of Dobruja, on the western shores of the Black Sea, who immigrated to the land of his ancestors in 1909.

Others joined the burgeoning Tatar nationalist movement, the so-called
Young Tatars, which looked to the Ottoman Young Turks for inspiration.
They were very radical and for this reason moved their base away from
any moderating influence Gaspirali might exert, to Karasubazar (now
Bilohirsk). This revolutionary organisation was run by Nurlu Kabirler
Abdürreşid Mehdi and had links to the Russian Socialist Party. After the
establishment of the Russian Duma (parliament) in St Petersburg, he took
his seat in 1907 – with the help of the liberal Kadet Party – and, in
concert with pro-autonomy delegates from Ukraine through the
Autonomists' Union, took an increasingly active role in Russian politics.
They published the Crimean Tatar newspaper *Servant of the Fatherland*,
whose editor-in-chief was Abdürreşid Mehdi. This earned him the
disgruntlement of Gaspirali who himself had hoped to be elected. Even
more radical was the secret organisation founded in Constantinople in
1909, by students Chelebi-Jihan and Jafer Seydamet. Known as Homeland,
its aim was Crimean independence, but its support was limited. Many
Crimeans were more interested, however, in the modest goals of the
newly-founded Crimean Tatar political party, *Melli Friqa* (National Party).
This was disturbing to the imperial authorities, even though the goals of
these Tatars were not aimed at political autonomy or a union with the
Ottoman Empire, since it encouraged the goal of achieving the
're-Islamisation' of Crimea, in particular, the introduction of Sharia Law.
As such, it turned its back on any pan-Turkic movement and focused
instead exclusively on Tatar-Turkic peoples residing within the Russian
Empire. It also lobbied for the requisition of former Tatar lands. Yet none
of these organisations succeeded in implementing any of their intended
goals and Tatar militancy failed to achieve any fruition until the advent of
the outbreak of the Russian February Revolution in 1917, and even then
the ethnic and religious focus of their campaign did not dovetail with the
views of 'class struggle' which the revolutionary parties of Russia were
increasingly supporting by the gun.

The highest levels of the Russian Tatar elite, long intermarried with
other Russian aristocrats, however, remained devoted to the tsar. For
them, Crimea was of primary interest as a pleasure resort during the
warmer months. For example, Sokolyne (Kokközy) the new hunting lodge
of the princely Yusopov family, themselves of Tatar, though not Crimean,

origins, was built between 1908–10 by the architect Nikolai Krasnov, with Crimean Tatar themes and decorative features, one of a number of such pleasure palaces to take inspiration from the Crimean Tatar past.

Massandra Palace and Estate

The late nineteenth and early twentieth centuries witnessed a final flowering of palatial imperial architecture in Crimea before the outbreak of the First World War, and the Revolution thereafter led to its abrupt end. In primary place was the construction of the imperial palace of Massandra, built in two bursts, first in 1881–82, and then 1892–1902, by the architects Étienne Bouchard and Maximilian Messmacher.

Prince Mikhail Vorontsov, Governor of Crimea, had long wanted to develop the Massandra estate. However, this was only realised by his son Count Mikhail Vorontsov. Employing the architect Étienne Bouchard, he commenced the building of a palatial hunting lodge at Massandra in the style of a French Renaissance chateau, but he died before its completion. Then, in 1889, it was acquired on behalf of Tsar Alexander III who, nonetheless, preferred to continue to reside at the Livadia Palace. Upon the accession of Tsar Nicholas II, it became, in turn, his Crimean dacha. Later, during the Soviet period, it would accommodate a litany of premiers and powerful government figures, including Josef Stalin, Nikita Khrushchev, Leonid Brezhnev and finally Mikhail Gorbachev; since 1992, it has been open as an historic monument for the general public.

It was also at Massandra that Prince Lev Golitsyn (1845–1915) began the production of sweet Muscat-based wines from the 1890s, following in the footsteps of Georgy Khristoforo, a native of Crimea of Greek extraction, who had previously tried to revive local viniculture.

Another member of the imperial family, Prince Pyotr Nikolaevich, had the Dulber Palace (1895–97) built in an Islamic style which took inspiration from Moorish Spain rather than from anything in Tatar Crimea or the Ottoman Empire. Finally, there was the smaller Yusopov palace at Koreyiz (1909), also designed in an Islamic style.

Swallow's Nest

Industrial magnates also left their mark on Crimea in architectural terms, of which the Swallow's Nest – a small but incredibly picturesque castle in a style which looks to Neuschwannstein, in southern Germany, and other fantastical neo-Gothic creations of King Ludwig of Bavaria – is the prime example. It is situated on a cliff protruding over the sea at Ai-Todor, not far from Gaspra, a small town between Yalta and Alupka and was built by the oil king, Baron von Steingel for his mistress, to the designs of the Russian architect of British descent Leonid Sherwood (1871–1954). A Baltic German, although a Russian subject, he wisely sold it to a noted local restaurateur in 1914, on the eve of the outbreak of the First World War. It suffered grievously in an earthquake in 1927 and was closed for decades during most of the Soviet period. In more recent years, however, it has undergone various restorations, the latest in 2011 and can now be viewed.

Literary Silver Age

It was during this period that Crimea underwent a literary Silver Age, only surpassed by its Golden Age earlier in the nineteenth century. One of its leading figures was Stepan Rudansky (1834–73), a native of western Ukraine, who practised as a medical doctor in Yalta, after his studies in St Petersburg, but went on to become a significant humorist poet, despite his short life. His posthumous *Singing Rhymes* (1880) was highly popular because of the amusing but penetrating anecdotes it contained about a wide range of ethnic and religious communities within imperial Russia at that time. Other works by him, however, had tragic overtones, reflecting not only his own suffering from what was soon discovered to be a mortal illness, but the difficulties of life for many people in Russia at that time.

Another literary light was the Ukrainian poet Lesya Ukraïnka (real name, Larysa Petrivna Kosach-Kvitka; 1871–1913) who spent considerable time in Crimea during this period, as well as the Belorusian poet and novelist Maksim Bohdanovich (1891–1917), a native of Minsk, who also settled at Yalta. There he spent his final year vainly hoping to overcome tuberculosis, whilst enjoying considerable attention for his popular novel *Muzyka* (1908).

Crimean Art

Crimea also hosted a bevy of leading artists of the time. These included Arkhip Kuindzhi (1841–1910), one of the most famous of the artists to make their home in Crimea, a native of Ukraine, who had attended the Imperial Academy of Art in St Petersburg. His landscape works have a lyrical quality which seem to look to the Dutch seventeenth century artist van der Neer for inspiration. There was also Konstantin Bogayevsky (1872–1943), a native of Feodosia, who arguably became, the most important native Crimean painter.

Musical Life, the Theatre and other Developments

Musical life and the theatre also flourished in the pleasure resort which Crimea had become for Russia's rich and famous. The Armenian composer Alexander Spendiaryan (1871–1928) came to Crimea in the early twentieth century. There he produced his noted symphonic *Crimean Sketches* (First series, opus 9), which was published in 1903. From the world of the theatre, numerous international figures also arrived, among them, the world renowned Russian opera singer Fedor Shaliapin. He visited Crimea in 1916, when a famous portrait of him, together with the Russian authors Maxim Gorky and Stepan Skitalets (real name, Stepan Petrov) was painted during a visit to Foros, on the Crimean coast. It was carried out in the company of his close friend Gorky, with whom he later collaborated on a joint autobiography, the writing of which began in Crimea, in 1917.

Archaeological research in Crimea also enjoyed a wider fame, not least for research carried out by the archaeologist and numismatist Aleksandr Berte-Delagard (1842–1920), a native of Sevastopol. Yet it was in the realms of medical treatments and innovations that Crimea became most famous, enabling it to continue as the sanatorium of the Russian elite, a status it maintains to this day, only rivalled by that of Sochi. Sergei Botkin, Vladimir Dmitriev and Stepan Rudansky were amongst the major medical men of Crimea who endeavoured to radically improve the standard of health and hygiene there. In particular, though, they are noted for their development of a plethora of sanatoria and other health facilities, exploiting the local climate and natural resources, coupled with the latest advances in terms of medical treatment and procedures. Thus, at the advent of the Russian Revolution and Civil War, Crimea can be said to have achieved a prosperity for both the elite and the wider population not realised since its Tatar slave-raiding days.

FROM THE FIRST WORLD WAR TO SOVIET POWER

The Outbreak of the First World War

The Ottoman Empire – now dominated by the belligerent Young Turks, in particular, the Grand Vizier Talaat Pasha, Minister of War Enver Pasha and Naval minister Djemal Pasha, who had made a puppet of the sultan and penultimate caliph Mehmet V – began its assault on Russia even before its declaration of war and the revelation of its military alliance with Imperial Germany. In October 1914, both Sevastopol and Feodosia were bombarded. In response, Russia declared war. The sultan, personally reluctant, was then obliged, on 14 November, to declare jihad against what were now billed as the enemies of Islam. However, Crimea's role in the military action of the Great War now came to an abrupt end. No further international military campaigns were fought there (unlike the catastrophic activity of the Second World War), but rather its ports served as points of embarcation or places of convalescent refuge for Russian troops coming and going in all the directions from the zones of military engagement. Many refugees from the war zones, Armenians in particularly, also fled there, especially during the mass slaughter which wiped them out in their millions in areas on the eastern periphery of what was becoming the decomposing corpse of the Ottoman Empire. Greeks, too, followed in their wake, fleeing the ancient coast cities and towns in which they had lived for millennia.

Reactions in Crimea to the First World War

Within Crimea, after the outbreak of the First World War, military security and intelligence was of course increased and some Crimean Tatars became the object of suspicious scrutiny, their spiritual loyalty to the sultan as caliph, bringing into doubt, as it had done in the Crimean War, their commitment to the Russian state. However, few Tatars identified with the Ottomans, nor took the call to arms to which the declaration of jihad had exhorted them. On the contrary, Mufti Adil Mirza Karashaysky explicitly declared his loyalty, and that of his flock, to Russia and its tsar. In consequence, thousands of Crimean men enlisted. The Tatar elite, in particular, joined the Crimean Cavalry, which had been one of its crack military regiments since the Crimean War. Loyal throughout the early years of the war until the Russian Empire itself began to unravel, few of their number changed sides, other than those later Tatar prisoners-of-war in Austria-Hungary, who, under the influence of propaganda during their imprisonment, began to identify with a wider anti-Russian pan-Turkic identity.[1] Those Crimean Tatars who had already identified strongly with Ottomans from the beginning of the war were in any case promoting their views and anti-Russian values through the Fatherland Society which had been established in Constantinople in the pre-war years by Noman Chelebi-Jihan and Jafer Seydamet, who by now had been conscripted into the Russian army, while covertly encouraging a nationalist Crimean Tatar political identity. However, even without their active leadership, the society's propaganda exhorted the Tatars to resist by the creation of secret cells to undermine what they perceived as the tsarist regime occupying Crimea. By 1917, in the collapse of order in Crimea, so-called national councils were being formed to support Tatar national independence or at least autonomy. After the fall of the imperial government during the February Revolution of 1917 and the establishment of the provisional republican government, the moment looked auspicious for Crimean Tatar nationalists to seize power. In consequence, the Fatherland Society openly showed its face in Crimea and in March, in the administrative capital Simferopol it convoked an All Crimean Muslim Conference which drew its men from the previously secret cells established during the war in villages all over Crimea. However, the Provisional Government under its president Alexander Kerensky strongly disapproved and endeavoured to suppress its activities. Nonetheless, Chelebi-Jihan and Seydamet, carried on – the former having been released from military service and now democratically elected as mufti by the congress and both of whom had become leaders of the Provisional Crimean Muslim Executive Committee. By the summer of

1917, a new political party Mili Firka had been formed, but this was one in which both the Tatar clergy and elite were sidelined. For the new party had both a nationalist and a socialist agenda which envisioned the dispersal of land from the large estates to Tatar smallholders.

This reorientation of the Crimean political leadership to the left was strongly supported by Bolshevist leader Vladimir Lenin and the new Russian authorities in Petrograd after the success of the October Revolution, in 1917 even if their authority in Crimea at this stage was very limited. In consequence, a Crimean Tatar National Assembly was convoked at highly symbolic Bakhchisaray, the old Tatar capital (26 November–8 December 1917). A democratic constitution was adopted and five members, two of whom were Chelebi-Jihan and Seydamet, were chosen to join the National Directorate, or principal administrative organisation, to be established at Simferopol. The Crimean Democratic Republic was declared on 25 December that same year with the support of the Crimean Cavalry Regiment and, it was hoped, supported externally by what remained of the authority of the rapidly fading Ottoman imperial government.

However, the Crimean leadership and body politic was increasingly cloven by sharp internal rifts. Thus, as 1917 drew to a close, two rival governments, both at Simferopol, claimed authority over Crimea. One, the National Directorate, acted in the name of an independent Crimean Democratic Republic, the other, the Crimean Democratic Assembly, in that of a republican Crimea united to a democratic Russia. A powerful and more lasting organisation was to prove the real winner in this context: The Bolshevik Sevastopol Soviet. In December 1917 it set up REVKOM (Military Revolutionary Committee) which claimed authority over not only Crimea but the entire province of Taurida. Unlike the other two organisations, REVKOM was backed by the enlisted sailors of the Black Sea Fleet, who had mutinied in June 1917, drowning their officers in the harbour of Sevastopol. If Simferopol held aloof, Sevastopol, Feodosia and Kerch were theirs before the end of the year. Then, in January 1918, even Simferopol fell to the Taurida Military Revolutionary Committee. On 28–30 January it formulated its own governing council for the whole of the province. This put it in conflict with Kiev, now under the authority of the newly established government, the Central Rada, which had declared an independent Ukraine and, on 22 January, the annexation to it of Crimea.

In the vacuum created by these competing organisations, along with ever growing numbers of marauders and refugees fleeing the burgeoning upheavals which had destroyed the civil fabric of the Russian Empire, lawlessness and terror reigned. No one was safe in Crimea, least of all the old elite, whether members of the clergy or the land owning classes. Even Noman Chelebi-Jihan, the great symbol of Crimean nationhood, was not spared. However, his poem *I Pledge* has since become a veritable national anthem for Crimean Tatars and recently a statue has been erected to commemorate his memory. Yet the Taurida Soviet Socialist Republic, which had been proclaimed in March 1918 was also to prove ephemeral as well, surviving for no more than five weeks.

In late winter 1918, some Tatar leaders, fearsome of the new Bolshevik regime, approached the Imperial German government to come to their succour. Dovetailing with German interests, the latter sent their army into Crimea in April, along with a corps of Crimean Tatar exiles from the Balkans (Dobruja, in today's south-eastern Romania and north-eastern Bulgaria), led by the Lithuanian Karaite Tatar, General Matwiej Sulejman Sulkiewicz (there had been an established community in Lithuania since the early fourteenth century), who had formerly fought on behalf of Russia. The Ukrainian Rada in Kiev responded, ordering their military leader Colonel Petro Bolbochan to preserve Crimea as a Ukrainian territory. The Germans, however, proved too powerful, and the Ukrainians retired. The Bolsheviks, too, were forced into retreat, making their last stand at Yalta where, captured by the Germans, they were summarily executed. The collapse of the Taurida Soviet Republic by late April was complete.

Once again the Crimean Tatars formed a parliament. However, this was rapidly bypassed by the creation, in June 1918, of a new, albeit short lived, Crimean Regional Government, under General Sulkiewicz. With the departure of the Germans after the Armistice in November 1918, ending the First World War, its primary support collapsed. The White Russian forces under General Anton Denikin at first filled the vacuum, giving their support for leader to Soloman Krym (1867–1936), a Karaite landowner of considerable substance. Unable to consolidate local factions, some of whom favoured the Bolsheviks, whose military forces were approaching from the north, this government collapsed in April 1919. Civil War and instability then reigned. First, with the support of the Red Army, the Crimean Soviet

Socialist Republic was proclaimed on 29 April. None other than Dimitry Ulyanov, a younger brother of Lenin, was appointed its leader. Colonel Denikin, however, was not prepared to accept this as a fait accompli, and returned to Crimea with the White Army. The Ulyanov regime collapsed in early July. Denikin's Whites failed to bring stability, not least because they sought reprisals on Bolsheviks and on Crimean Tatars in general, many of whose loyalty to the Whites and a unified Russia had come to be doubted. In consequence, the Tatar nationalist Mili Firka Party formed its own guerrilla movement, known as the Green Bands, taking to militant opposition. However, this movement was itself fractured. Supporters under Jafar Seydamet had a fiercely nationalistic Crimean Tatar agenda, whilst those under Veli Ibrahimov had a more internationalist ideology which lent support to the Bolsheviks.

In late 1920, Baron Pyotr Wrangel assumed the leadership of White forces and, with respect to Crimea, brought with him a more inclusive agenda, which took greater account not only of Crimean Tatar nationalist aspirations, but of the demands of many poor farmers of various ethnicities for land reforms. However, it was a case of 'too little, too late': the Red army was once again on the march southwards, under the skilled leadership of Mikhail Frunze. Communist opposition also gathered strength under Nestor Makhno. Resistance collapsed and, by the beginning of November 1920, Crimea was overrun. The coastal cities and towns of the peninsula filled with refugees in flight creating a Boschian vision of hell. In particular, Feodosia, Kerch, Sevastopol and Yalta filled with Whites, soldiers and civilians, fleeing the imminent horrors of Bolshevik hegemony. No less than 144,000 thousand people – half military, half civilian – took flight on some 120 ships to any safe port that would take them, the exodus protected by the French navy based at Odessa.[2] (The Dowager Empress Maria Feodorovna, widow of Tsar Alexander III and mother of Tsar Nicholas II, who had earlier taken refuge with other family members in Crimea, had fled from Yalta the year before on the HMS Marlborough). On 14 November 1920, General Wrangel himself departed on the final cruiser from Sevastopol, and the great ship that was imperial Russia sank. The final subjugation of Crimea, indeed, all Russia, to the Bolsheviks was now complete.

The battle fought in Crimea in November 1920 proved conclusive. The White troops of Baron Wrangel then in control of Crimea were defeated by the victorious Red army. This event was later commemorated by the Russian composer Georgy Sviridov as the subject of choral songs in his *Oratorio of Pathos* (1959), based on poems by Vladimir Mayakovsky. They include, Tale of the Flight of General Wrangel' and 'To the Heroes of the Battles of Perikop.' In 1968, the Russian film director Yevgeny Karelov directed the film *Two Comrades were Serving* (1968) also on this subject.

Béla Kun and the Bolshevik Reign of Terror

In the middle of November 1920, the Red Army imposed the Crimean Revolutionary Committee's authority over all of Crimea. Béla Kun, whose name was a byword for terror from his brief rule over his native Hungary's short lived Soviet Republic (1919), was given supreme command, as a leading member of the Military Council of the Red Army of the Southern Front. During the following months a reign of terror, indeed, a bloodbath, ensued the likes of which Crimea had never before experienced. No less than between 50,000 to 100,000 men, women and even children, were condemned as enemies of the people.[3] These were now summarily executed, some beheaded. Even some of the most committed Bolsheviks were shocked by these circumstances and one influential Volga Tatar, Mir Sultan-Galiev, who formulated the ideology of Muslim 'nationalist' Communism, condemned Béla and his henchmen for their excesses to Moscow. The reality was, however, that it was the notorious secret police, the Cheka, established in 1917, who had facilitated these massacres, rather than merely Kun.

The Establishment of the Crimean Autonomous Socialist Republic

The Russian Soviet Federative Socialist Republic had been established on 7 November 1917. However, it was first on 18 October 1921 that the subsidiary Crimean Autonomous Soviet Socialist Republic was founded. It consisted of a praesidium of five members, supported by a soviet of fifteen so-called people's commissars. Rather than being attached to Soviet Ukraine, though, it was attached directly to Russia, or to be precise, what was now the Russian Federative Soviet Socialist Republic. This was the beginning of a new, ultimately terrible, epoch.

Tatar Rehabilitation during the 1920s

As a result of wars, revolutions, famine and disease, massive changes were wrought in the ethnic composition of Crimea by the time of the census of 1926: Russians were in the majority now, some 301,000, compared with Crimean Tatars, who, with only 179,000 now formed only a quarter of the population. Ukrainians had greatly increased in number to 77,000, but most significant was the presence of 44,000 Germans and 40,000 Ashkenazi Jews. The centuries old communities of Krymchak Tatars (also Jewish) now counted 6,000 in size, the Greeks 16,000, Armenians and Bulgarians 11,000 each and the Karaites 8,000. The remaining 20,000 were of a wide variety of nationalities.[4]

The Tatars had suffered severely during the era of Béla Kun. However, in the years which followed when Soviet rule over Crimea was consolidated, their lot improved dramatically. Indeed, as the Canadian historian Paul Robert Magocsi has put it,

> The Crimean Tatars became the dominant political and socioeconomic force in the Crimean ASSR. …as a group they were assigned the largest number of self-governing village soviets: 144 Crimean Tatar as compared to 106 for the Russians and only 3 for Ukrainians.[5]

Now, too, the return of Tatar refugees came to be encouraged, especially for those who had fled to Turkey during the worst years of the Civil War. They were granted an amnesty and many returned 'home', this immigration, in a small way, compensating for the loss of just over a fifth of the population since pre-war days.

A former leading figure of the Crimean Tatar National Party (Mili Firka), Veli Ibrahimov facilitated this positive transformation of Tatar life in Crimea. He combined his newly acquired credentials as a Bolshevik with those of a Tatar nationalist in a manner which made him popular, not only in Crimea, but far more importantly, in Moscow. For that reason, he became Crimea's uncontested despot, chairman of the Central Committee of the Communist Party of Crimea and Council of People's Commissars. At the same time, he showed no hesitation in implementing reforms – although some ardent Bolsheviks lamented them as accommodations with capitalism – such as the New Economic Policy (NEP), which legally permitted, sometimes encouraged, small scale market activity throughout the Soviet Union.

Tatar identity, along with its growing economic and political influence strengthened at this time. Having grown now to a quarter of the peninsula's population, their share of the membership in the party and various government bodies grew from 30 to 60 per cent.[6]

Ibrahimov's star, however, was to prove short-lived in the Soviet firmament. Overestimating the respect he commanded in Moscow, he vociferously objected to Moscow's plan to resettle many Jews from the former Pale of Settlement, in the west of Russia, to Crimea. However, his voice was ignored and more than 5,100 Ashkenazi Jews were settled there in the 1920s, most in agricultural areas in the northern interior steppes zone – by contrast to those who had arrived thirty and forty years before and had settled in the major cities. Two Jewish Crimean nationality districts were specifically created for them: Fraidorf and Larindorf. However, their establishment in these areas proved short lived, in the wake of the implementation of the agricultural collectivisation of the early 1930s. Many Jews then moved to cities and towns, much as they had done before. However, their population continued to grow, so that, by the eve of the Second World War, no less than 60,000 were residing in Crimea.[7]

Ibrahimov's fall was swift and, in 1928, he was condemned for bourgeois nationalism and executed, not an unusual fate for many old Bolsheviks who increasingly over the following decade fell foul of the Soviet regime, sometimes for no obvious reason.

He was not alone even then amongst the Tatars. Soon, some 3,500 of them, members of government, as well as literati, amongst them, Bekir Chobanzade (1893–1937), and Shevki Bektöre, were arrested. The lucky were sent into exile, the unlucky shot.[8]

Matters worsened during the course of the 1930s, reaching a crescendo all over the Soviet Union in the late 1930s. Chobanzade was just one such murdered during these purges. (A commemorative monument has recently been erected to his memory in his native Karasubazar (now Bilohirsk).

By 1936 a Moscow directed campaign was firmly underway to crush Crimean Tatar identity and to impose Russian culture and language upon them. Already in 1929, the Latin alphabet had been imposed over the Arabic one for the Crimean Tatar language. Tatar newspapers and journals were also gradually suppressed, then dramatically reduced, from twenty-three in 1935, to only nine in 1938. Those who persisted in advocating not only the medium of the Arabic alphabet, but the Latin one as well, now came to be viewed by the Soviet authorities as enemies of the state – only the Cyrillic one was now deemed to be politically acceptable. Those who objected were frequently accused of bourgeois nationalism, and suffered the death penalty which was usually meted out for 'serious crimes' against the state. Many Tatar cultural activities were banned and the National Theatre closed.

Religious Persecution

Already from the beginning of the Soviet period, the Russian Orthodox Church, long established in pre-revolutionary imperial days, lost not only its official status and landed property but its icons and liturgical implements, vessels and books. Indeed, it also lost most of its priests and monks, either murdered, imprisoned or deported. Gold items in church were confiscated and melted down, against the backdrop of the martyrdom of Tikhon, Patriarch of All Russia, himself, on 25 March 1925. He had previously been Bishop of Alaska and primate of the Russian Orthodox Church in America, in which capacity he travelled throughout the United States, during the early years of the century, consecrating numerous churches and some monastic houses. He is a highly revered figure there, even to this day.

The Orthodox were not alone in suffering persecution. A similar fate was to await the ulema of the Muslim community as well, only later. In Crimea, after the initial pogroms against all clergy by the Bolsheviks during the Civil War, a certain degree of toleration had come to be respected by the Soviet authorities. However, with the loss by the Tatars of their formerly, albeit brief, privileged status, the persecutions were renewed with fresh vigour. In consequence, from 1931–35, the mosques of Crimea were shut, many of their clergy murdered or deported to Siberia. The terror reached its height in 1935–37, when more than 3,000 people were arrested, of whom 400 were accused of foreign espionage or other forms of counter-revolutionary activities, often linked to foreign powers like Nazi Germany.

Consolidations of the 1930s

By 1930, the Armenian community in Crimea had also suffered severe depredations. There were then only some 13,000 Armenians living in two Armenian national districts in the republic, a considerable drop from the almost 17,000 said to be living there in 1919.[10]

The Jewish Krymchaks (some said to be descended from those who settled in Crimea in the classical period, i.e. first century BC to seventh century AD), on the other hand, increased during the interwar period,. Their version of Tatar being taught at their schools well into the 1920s. In 1897, there were said to be some 3,500 living in Crimea, many in and around Karasubazar (Bilohersk), where they had been living since the sixteenth century. At the start of the Second World War, their numbers had almost doubled to 6,500, just before the annihilation imposed upon them by Nazi German occupying forces during that war.[11]

Industrial Collapse, Revival and Development

In the wake of the Russian revolutions and the ensuing civil war, Crimea's industrial infrastructure had virtually collapsed. The factories of Sevastopol, Kerch and other cities of Crimea had simply ceased to function. But after the advent of NEP, matters improved dramatically. Later the three five-year plans which sought to bring the Soviet Union in line with other major world powerhouse states also brought further industrial development. Thus, the 1930s in Crimea witnessed an upsurge which definitively made it a powerhouse of heavy industry. The Voikov Metallurgy Factory and the Dzhanko Electro-energy Power Station were just two examples of such endeavours constructed at this time and numerous others followed in their train.

Educational Developments

Mass education also underwent a boom. An extension of literacy and education was a very important element in the Soviet development of all areas of the country and especially so in Crimea. Thus, by 1930, hundreds of new schools were established and Tatar children benefited, at least in the beginning, particularly. No less than 387 primary schools had been established by that year specifically for them. The language of instruction was in Tatar, using the traditional Arabic alphabet which had been used since the conversion of the Turks and Tatars to Islam, at a time when it was forbidden in Turkey itself where the Latin alphabet was now in use. The newly founded Crimean State Publishing House provided a wide range of books and other printed matter to support this development. Taurida University, Crimea's first, had been founded during the upheavals of 1918, at Simferopol, and it was now expanded. This was soon followed by no less than four other universities and polytechnics, not to mention forty technical colleges. These developments in education were as important as the five-year plans. In consequence, a population in which the majority had been illiterate achieved 97 per cent literacy by 1934.[12]

Development of Agriculture

The miseries befalling Crimea in the early post-war period were increased exponentially by natural calamities. A drought of almost biblical proportions afflicted the peninsula during the summer growing season of 1921. In consequence, famine and the epidemics which followed in its wake led to the death of some 60 to 70 per cent of the entire population, between 100,000 and 110,000 people, but with the greatest impact being on the Crimean Tatars who resided in the poorest and least agriculturally productive steppes and central mountains. Almost half the population of Bakhchisaray starved to death, and by 1923 a mere quarter of the Crimean population was Tatar.

Just as industry had suffered a complete collapse after the war, so agricultural production had virtually ceased after the military, political and social upheavals which had befallen Crimea. This was aggravated by the fact that the landed estates of Crimea were rapidly formed by the Soviet authorities into state run farms, organised along the lines of forced collectivisation. This was generally abhorred by the peasantry which had expected the great estates to be divided up, individual parcels from which they thought would be allotted to individual peasants and their families. Thus, these collective farms, known under the acronym SOVHOZ, met with great resistance but to no avail. By the spring of 1921, over a quarter of Crimea's farmland was absorbed into SOVHOZ, with 45 per cent of orchards and vineyards similarly collectivised.[13]

Nonetheless, these difficulties notwithstanding, Crimean agriculture revived. In particular, tobacco and fruit became increasingly important commodities and it was in these industries, especially in the former, that the newly arriving Jews from the west were invited to participate.

Despite the increasing productivity of agriculture, the collectivisation of farming continued to be highly unpopular, especially after it drew to a close in 1931. This was especially the case amongst the Tatars, who committed many acts of sabotage to hinder its implementation and continuation. Crops were not sown; livestock was killed to prevent the state benefiting from them. In consequence, the Soviet authorities turned their malevolent eyes upon them. The honeymoon of the Crimean Tatars with the Soviet authorities drew to an abrupt and brutal close. In 1928–29, 35,000 to 40,000 Tatar farming people were exiled to the central Asian Soviet republics.[14] Then, in December 1930, a serious revolt broke out at Alakat amongst those still in Crimea, and the deportations were renewed. This encouraged food shortages, albeit not to the degree of the wider Ukrainian Holodomor, that deliberately induced famine in which millions of peasants perished.

In any case, new immigrants arrived in vast numbers to take the place of those deported, dead or imprisoned. As a result of this vast new immigration, Crimea's agricultural food production continued to grow. Grain, fruit and wine, the latter on large state collectives, rather than smaller village ones, doubled in quantity compared to that of pre-war levels.[15]

The Palaces, Mansions and Parks Reinvented

The Soviet authorities rejected as abhorrent many material aspects of the old discredited Imperial regime. However, this did not prevent them from appreciating the magnificent palaces and delightful villas which had been the hallmark of that system. Therefore, the grandest of the imperial palaces and mansions of pre-Revolutionary Crimea were reinvented as residences for Communist leaders and other officials, as well as for important foreign visitors, whether fellow-travellers or even capitalists.

Koreyiz, the palatial residence of the princely Yusopov family, built by the architect Nikolai Krasnov in 1909, was one such. It was frequently visited by members of the Communist International during the interwar years. The Naryshkin Mansion, which had earlier in the nineteenth century been in the possession of the Vorontsovs and Bobrinskys, was nationalised and given over to the Department of Forestry, under the direction of the noted Professor Morozov, whilst, in 1920, the Salgirka Park became a plant reserve. The Crimean Agricultural Institute was granted jurisdiction there and eventually it was transferred to the State Institute for Viniculture.

Crimean Literature

Literature thrived during the interwar years in Crimea, in spite of or perhaps because of the hardships endured. There were, of course, the greats, Maxim Gorky and Vladimir Mayakovsky, but lesser stars of note also worked there, some focusing on specifically Crimean subject matter. These include Alexander Grin, Sergei Sergeev-Tsenskiy and Konstantin Treniëv, who were amongst the most noted members of the Union of Writers of Crimea, a Soviet literary umbrella organisation. Possibly its most eccentric member – but surprisingly well tolerated, even lauded by the Soviet authorities and Stalin – was Maximilian Voloshin (1877–1932). This Symbolist painter, poet and philosopher was a native of Kiev, who settled in the tourist resort of Koktebel in Crimea, where his house became a centre of artistic pilgrimage and which even today is an important museum dedicated to his memory and the focus of much artistic and literary activity.

The Arts against a Backdrop of Collectivisation, Deportation and Famine

Despite the deaths of millions during the Civil War and Holodomor, the painterly arts continued to be favoured and were actively encouraged by the Soviet authorities, indeed, even by Stalin himself. Socialist realism may have been the official style which Soviet theory demanded, but in Crimea, romanticism still held sway. The Crimean landscapes of the 1930s by Konstantin Bogayevsky (1872–1943) still have a Claudian atmosphere which gives no hint of the horrors which stalked the peninsula from the period of the Civil War in the early 1920s to the Second World War and beyond. Bogayevsky had studied at the Russian Imperial Academy of Art where the great Ukrainian artist Arkhip Kuindzhi, a member of the famous Slavic and Realist inspired Travellers Movement, had been his professor. However, he had settled in Crimea at the beginning of the twentieth century and devoted himself thereafter to the depiction of its eastern rugged coast, becoming a founding member of the so-called Cimmerian stylistic school of art (the name derives from the ancient Greek name for the eastern Crimean coastal area).

Also of note was the Ukrainian artist Mykola Samokysh (1860–1944) who moved to Crimea from Nizhyn, in Russia, and who had also attended the Russian Imperial Academy of Art in St Petersburg. He became a leading artist of the interwar years focusing on historic military scenes, and enjoyed the favour of Stalin who awarded him the coveted Stalin Prize in 1941. However, the sudden unexpected attack on Russia by Nazi Germany, the Molotov Pact notwithstanding, was to change the focus of the Soviet authorities.

THE SECOND WORLD WAR, YALTA,
AND THE POST-WAR SETTLEMENT

Nazi Germany and the Crimean Campaign

In April 1941, two months before Germany's invasion of the Soviet Union, it was agreed by the Nazi regime that Crimea should be separated from Russia and ceded to a puppet Ukrainian pro-German state. In July, when the German armies were already penetrating deep into Soviet territory, Adolph Hitler himself chaired a meeting on Crimean policy at which this so-called 'Gotenland' project was in principle accepted. As for the Crimean Tatars, they were judged to be racially worthless – like the Jews – but their deportation would be delayed in order not to offend neutral Turkey, to whom they were ethnically related. The Soviets, anticipating the invasion, had already rounded up the old German population of Crimea, some 61,000 people, in August 1941. They were deported to Stavropol and its environs, in the interior of Caucasus, across the Sea of Kerch, to the east.[1]

Meanwhile, on 4 August, Hitler arrived at Novy Borissov, where he expounded on the primary importance of seizing Crimea out of fear that a failure to do so would ensure that the peninsula could become a veritable 'Soviet aircraft carrier operating against the Romanian oilfields.'[2] Then, on 21 August, Hitler communicated to his commander General Field Marshal Fedor von Bock his Crimean priorities:

> The army's proposal for the continuation of the operations…does not correspond with my plans. I order the following… The most important objective to be achieved before the onset of winter is not the occupation of Moscow, but the taking of the Crimea, the industrial and coal region of the Donetsk Basin and the severing of Russian oil deliveries from the Caucasus area, in the north the encirclement of Leningrad and link-up with the Finns.[3]

CRIMEA

German Field Marshal Gerd von Rundstedt's 11th Army, supported by their Romanian ally with their 3rd and 4th armies, broke into Crimea in September 1941. By late October 1941, German armies, Operation Trappenjagd (Bustard Hunt) had succeeded so well that all but Sevastopol had capitulated. This had been made possible by Germany's great military strategist Field Marshal Erich von Manstein, whose so-called 'Sickle Cut' attack plan in France and Ukraine had proved so successful, even if Stalingrad itself had proven such a calamity. The Soviet General Ivan Petrov and his forces carried on their defence for a further eight months, with horrendous casualties. Military action around Balaklava took a terrible toll on them. Then, finally, Sevastopol, reduced to ruins, was overrun. All of Crimea was now in German hands. However, the departing Soviet forces made sure that what remained of their industrial and logistical infrastructure would provide the invaders with little benefit, as food stuffs were destroyed, the electrical network, telephone infrastructure and water purveyance all undone. Enemies of the Soviet state, whether in or out of prison, were immediately executed, to prevent them from assisting the Germans.

A ceremony marking the successful completion of the German Crimean Campaign (1941–1942), with the capture of Sevastopol by the German 11th Army under the command of General Erich von Manstein, and Manstein's promotion to the rank of Generalfeldmarschall (Field Marshal), was held in the garden of Livadia Palace on July 6, 1942, the most honoured amongst them awarded the Ritterkreuz (Knight's Cross) and gold Deutsches Kreuz (German Cross).

Crimea was annexed to the Reichskommissariat Ukraine as the Generalbezirk Krim and became an important testing ground for Aryanisation and German resettlement by the Nazi regime. This was to have mortal consequences for some of the ethnic communities, in particular, the Jews.

The Final Solution in Crimea

With the approach of the Germans to Crimea, many Jews fled elsewhere into less immediately threatened areas of the Soviet Union. However, many Jews were trapped and, after, the consolidation of power by the Nazi occupying forces during the autumn of 1941, they were rounded up much as they were elsewhere in Europe after German occupation. Rather than send them to Auschwitz or other extermination camps far away to the west, they were slaughtered on the spot. This was the case in Feodosia in December 1941. Summoned from the city and its environs for 'resettlement', all, regardless of sex or age, were murdered. So efficiently was this carried out that by April 1942, Crimea joined Estonia as a land declared by the Nazis 'Juden Frei' (Free of Jews).

Idiosyncratically, the National Socialists in Germany in 1935, had concluded that the non-Talmudic Jewish Karaites, in Crimea, Lithuania and elsewhere, were not racially Jewish. Therefore, after the invasion of Crimea, Hitler declared that they were not to be molested. In consequence, most Karaites supported or at least tolerated the Germans, some even serving as volunteers in the German military and administration. That said, as the war continued, some members of the SS lost the ability to distinguish them from other Jews with predictable fatal consequences.

Gotenland

As a new Aryan colonial territory of Nazi Germany, Crimea was renamed Gotenland, in honour of the ancient Goths, considered a paleo-Germanic people. The old capital Simferopol was renamed Gotenberg, Sevastopol, with its naval base, Theodorichhafen. The ideology of this plan was bolstered by the belief that Aryan immigrants from the German speaking Alto Adige (Southern Tirol), lost by Austria to Italy after the First World War, were descendants of these paleo-Germanic peoples, who had originally migrated there in the late first century BC. Benito Mussolini, il Duce of Fascist Italy, which belatedly had allied itself with Nazi Germany, was content to support this fiction, realising that their presence in the Alto Adige would otherwise leave an ethnic Trojan horse there, preventing, in the long term, Italy from reclaiming the now German province (Austria had been annexed to Germany through the Anschluss in March 1938). The war notwithstanding, archaeological investigations in Crimea were carried out to 'expose' its Gothic connections. This so-called Gotenland Project focused predominantly on what were presumed to be the ancient Gothic fortifications in and around the coastal towns of Inkerman, Alushta and Gurzuf. That said, it was Mangup, the old capital of the ancient Gothic Kingdom of Theodoro, which most interested them, with its great hilltop fortress. Needless to say, not only Jews, but Slavs and Tatar peoples ultimately had no place in this Gothic new world. On the other hand, wartime exigences prevented the actual arrival of any 'neo-Goths' from Alto Adige. Also of importance was the fact that the German occupation forces and their military commanders – initially General Rudstedt and then his successor Field Marshal Erich von Manstein – in no way wished to damage their relationship with Turkey, a country whose neutrality served German interests. This gave the Crimean Tatars a certain degree of protection.

The Tatars in the Wake of the German Occupation

Early on in the occupation, Field Marshal von Rudstedt and then von Manstein endeavoured to exploit the nascent hostility to Soviet rule which some Tatars maintained, in particular, those who had fled to Turkey, such as Jafar Seydamet and Edige Kirimli, or to Romania, such as Mustejip Ülküsal. Since the German occupation in 1918 had proven popular amongst many Tatars, the Germans were able to exploit its memory. They also acted as useful pawns of the Germans in their role as go-betweens for those Crimean Tatar Soviet soldiers who had fallen into the hands of the occupiers – altogether some 90,000 Soviet soldiers had been captured. These Tatar leaders also served a useful purpose in convincing some of the Tatar soldiers to change sides. By winter 1942, no less than 8,700 released from POW camps had joined the Wehrmacht. Moreover, even by late autumn 1941, there were some 6,000 Crimean Tatar volunteers, from more than 200 villages, who formed, amongst others, so-called police self-defence units fighting allied to the German occupiers. Even the SS now did not hesitate to solicit the Tatars, 1,600 of whom joined their ranks in special battalions or those of the supporting Tatar police units who did their bidding.[4]

Tatar civil and spiritual authorities were also wooed. To this end Alfred Frauenfeld, of the Reichskommissariat, facilitated the establishment of a Muslim Committee in Simferopol, in November 1941, which exerted its authority throughout Crimea, some of them including survivors from the pre-1917 nationalist parties, and a largely symbolic Tatar mission was established in Berlin. The German civil administration also followed this pro-Tatar line. The General Commissar, Frauenfeld, fell in love with the notion of restoring the Crimean Tatars as a Kulturvolk, that is, an ethnos of high culture. He reopened Tatar schools, functioning again for the first time in many years, and spent considerable resources on fostering Tatar language and customs. Expressions of Tatar culture were now encouraged: the Tatar National Theatre was reopened, whilst a Tatar language newspaper, *Azat Kirim* (Free Crimea, 1942–44), was published in sizeable numbers. There was also a scheme for establishing a Tatar university. Ultimately, however, these sops for attracting Tatar support completely contradicted the underlying Nazi ideology which had led to the creation of the Gotenland project.

A third policy began to emerge after the arrival of German troops and the pacification of Crimea, with the implementation of the SS command structure headed by Otto Ohlendorf. Racial and political extermination squads under SS command usually followed in the wake of the Wehrmacht (general army) in newly occupied areas. This was the case with the Einsatzgruppe D of the SS which ordered the execution by firing squad of 'undesirable elements'. The savageries of the SS drove more and more Tatars to join the partisans, or, where the Soviet guerrillas would not accept them, to form resistance groups of their own. By the time that the Red Army re-entered Crimea in April 1944, Ohlendorf had murdered some 130,000 people, including the entire gypsy population of Crimea, the remaining Jews and – disregarding those ethnological points so nicely made in Berlin – most of the Karaites. Tens of thousands of Tatars were among Ohlendorf's victims.

The Collapse of German Occupation

The Battle for Stalingrad, in January 1943, had signalled the turn of the tide with respect to the German occupation. In November of that same year, Soviet troops had spread southwards reaching the gateway to Crimea, Perekop. Hitler's exhortations to his commanders never to abandon the peninsula proved to be in vain. In April 1944, Soviet forces approached Crimea from the north and the east. Nazi Germany's last stand at Sevastopol also proved futile. Soviet troops entered the old Russian fortress city as victors on 12 May 1944. When the authorities took stock of the damaged infrastructure, the cost of the occupation became all to obvious. They discovered that even buildings belonging to the State Institutes of Agriculture and of Viniculture had been pillaged for much of their equipment which had been transferred back to Germany in the spring of 1944 in the wake of the Nazi retreat. That said, others of little industrial value, such as the Naryshkin Mansion, had escaped destruction by bombing or demolition. Alas, many of the inhabitants of Crimea fared less well than its material infrastructure both during and after the war.

Deportation of the Crimean Tatars

At first, the executions and deportations in Crimea primarily impacted Jews, both newly established Ashkenazi as well as anciently established Krymchaks. Of these, no less than 40,000 were murdered by summer 1942. Non Jewish Russians also suffered. 13,000 of whom were executed, including some Tatars. Others were spared their lives but a further 85,000 – mainly Russian – were deported as prisoner workers to serve the Reich. Even the physical infrastructure of domestic life was disrupted, with at least a hundred villages in Crimea put to the torch.[5]

Soviet activity to undermine the German occupation of Crimea persisted even during the worst days of Nazi control. Indeed, partisans saw it as one of their important activities. To this end, they carried out the execution of those, in particular, Crimean Tatars, who sided with the Germans. The collateral damage was occasionally deliberate, after the reoccupation of Crimea by the Soviets in April 1944, with whole Tatar villages being slaughtered. Sometimes, even Tatars who volunteered for the Soviet partisans were not spared although perhaps as many as 20,000 ordinary Crimean Tatar soldiers did carry on fighting in the Soviet army, not only in Crimea but elsewhere on the front.[6] Thousands of them were honoured for bravery, with eight awarded the Soviet Union's greatest medal – that of the Hero of the Soviet Union. One such was the famed Tatar Soviet Air Force pilot, Akhmetkhan Sultan (1920–70), who was awarded this medal twice.

From 1941 other Tatars, unwelcome in the wider partisan movement formed their own anti-German units. These were said to number 630, out of a partisan total of 3,783. Thus, Crimean Tatars formed 16.6 per cent of all partisans there. That figure was low bearing in mind that 19.3 per cent of the total pre-war population was Crimean Tatar.[7] The fact remained, that most militarily active Tatars provided help to the Germans. As Soviet partisan commander Aleksey Mokrousov put it at the time: 'The overwhelming majority of the Crimean Tatars who live in the mountains and foothills have given their support to the Fascists.'[8]

It is no surprise then that both the Soviet partisans and the government took severe actions to deal with them, irrespective of the fact that many Tatars increasingly changed sides as more and more became aware that a German defeat was imminent. 18 May 1944 – known even now as 'The Black Day', turned out to be the key date in the implementation of Stalin's Tatar Soviet policy: the deportation to central Asia of all of the Crimean Tatars, irrespective of age, sex or political convictions held. This was the penalty imposed for what the supreme Soviet leader perceived as their collective and unforgivable betrayal. The Tatars were given one hour each to appear for resettlement. Three days later, the deportation of some 183,200 had been accomplished and by 9 June this number increased to 188,600.[9] Ultimately, between September 1941 and November 1944, more than 220,000 Crimean Tatars were deported by the NKVD (Soviet Secret Police) who oversaw the enforcement of the deportation, under the watchful eyes of its director Lavrenty Beria. Within a few days, Crimea had been emptied of Tatars, transported in cattle cars, devoid of sanitary or other forms of logistical infrastructure, northwards and eastwards to Siberia and Kazakhstan. As a result, they died in their thousands in transport, especially babies and the elderly.

A Russian who observed the deportation noted:

> It was a journey of lingering death in cattle railway cars, crammed with people, like mobile gas chambers. … Death mowed down the old, the young and the weak. They died of thirst, suffocation, and the stench.

> On the long stages the corpses decomposed in the middle of the cattle cars and at the short halts, where water and food were handed out, the people were not allowed to bury their dead and had to leave them beside the railway track.

About 151,000 Crimean Tatars were eventually resettled in the Uzbek SSR, while most of the remainder were sent to the Udmurt and Mari oblasts of the Russian SFSR. There they were resettled on land unable to sustain them, with little supporting infrastructure. They died in their thousands as a result. Only decades later, during the declining final decades of the Soviet period, were some able to make their way back to Crimea. Most Crimean Tatars, therefore, remained in their internal exile even in the late 1980s. With the growing *perestroika* which allowed the rumblings of dissent and discontent to increasingly make itself heard without fear of major repressions, the Crimean Tatars became so bold as to hold a seated demonstration in July 1987 in Red Square, in Moscow, demanding the right of return to Crimea.

The ethnic cleansing of the Crimean Tatars on the peninsula had a scorpion-like sting in its tail though, with respect to Soviet troops there. For it had been left to Soviet soldiers to harvest the crops of Crimea during the summers of 1944 and 1945. No less than 200 of them fell victim to a terrible visitation of haemorrhagic fever, a tick borne illness indigenous to equatorial Africa but occasionally found in south-eastern Europe.

The Crimean Tatars were the first Soviet ethnic minority to suffer total deportation. A few weeks after Soviet power had been re-established in Crimea, the entire remaining Crimean Tatar population was expelled to Central Asia. Only two years later was this deportation made public. First in 1956 when Nikita Khrushchev, who had assumed the premiership after Stalin's death in 1953, publicly discussed and denounced the Tatar deportation. This he did in an anti-Stalin speech presented at the Twentieth Party Congress, after petitions had arrived in Moscow from the Crimean Tatar diaspora in Tashkent.

Deportation of Armenians, Bulgarians and Greeks

The Tatars were not the only residents of Crimea to suffer deportation. On the eve of the Second World War, Armenians formed one of Crimea's largest minorities. In fact, in Feodosia, more than 20 per cent of the population was said to be Armenian.[11] However, on 29 May 1944, Lavrenty Beria initiated the decimation and deportation of the Armenians in Crimea. Inciting Stalin's innate paranoid fears of the danger posed by non-Russian and Georgian peoples within the Soviet Union, he warned the Soviet leader that Armenians, along with Crimean Bulgarians and Greeks, were siding with the Nazis. This was followed on 2 June by the so-called Directorate 5984 (Deportation of German Satellites) which ordered the deportation of Crimea's Armenians to far flung reaches of the Soviet

Union, in particular, to Kazakhstan and Bashkortostan, in the Asiatic heartlands to the east, Tatarstan around Kazan (between the Urals and Moscow), to the Urals, around today's Ekaterinenburg (then Sverdlovsk) and to the Arctic north in the Perm region. Altogether some 37,000 people of these three ethnic groups were deported.[12] From June 1944, the figures for those deported work out as follows: Armenians (9,800), Bulgarians (12,600), and Greeks (16,000).[13] All in all, the Soviets deported more than 288,000 Crimeans of diverse ethnicities by 1944.[14] This total includes the 438 Crimean Italians whom the Soviet Army deported to Kazakhstan from eastern Crimea in 1942.[15]

The Yalta Conference

From 4 to 11 February 1945, the Crimean Conference took place at the old imperial Crimean resort of Yalta, in which US president Franklin D. Roosevelt, British prime minister Winston Churchill and Soviet leader Joseph Stalin, came to an arrangement over the defeat of Nazi Germany and the post-war settlement. Roosevelt was allotted the Livadia Palace, convenient to the less mobile president, since it was also the venue for the conference. Churchill was given the Vorontsov Palace, at Alpuka, with all its historical British associations. Stalin himself stayed at the Yusopov Palace in Koreyiz.

Already for some time in late 1944, the Allies were convinced that the war in Europe would soon be over. Though they were also of the opinion that the war in east Asia and the Pacific would drag on. Therefore, it became of great importance to the western Allies that the Soviet Union, which had held aloof on this front, now join in on the Japanese kill. Political carrots had consequently to be extended to Stalin to convince him of the wisdom and practical benefits of so doing. Therefore, they offered: Manchuria (control of the railways and other economic benefits); former imperial Russian Port Arthur (now Lüshunko, a very favourable leasehold); the southern half of Sakhalin (Japanese since the Russo-Japanese War of 1905) and also the northern Japanese Kurile Islands.

As for Europe itself, it was acknowledged that the countries of eastern Europe adjacent to the Soviet Union would also fall under its sphere of influence, though not to the degree – it was naively thought – that democratic elections would be impaired. One sour note which had to be accepted, was that Communists in Poland would be guaranteed a political voice there. The newly projected United Nations also came into focus, since all the parties at the conference, with the addition of France, would have the right of veto on the powerful Security Council, in which ultimate authority lay.

Re-establishment of Soviet Crimea

On 30 June 1945 the Crimean Autonomous Soviet Socialist Republic first created in 1921, was abolished. Now Crimea was re-established as one of the many administrative regions or *oblast* of the Russian Soviet Federative Socialist Republic, its ancient Crimean Tatar identity largely effaced, as Slavic names – first Russian, then Ukrainian – replaced Tatar ones. New peoples from outside the region were also brought in to replenish its highly depleted population. Sevastopol and Kerch, which had boasted populations of over 100,000 each before the war, now had a mere 1,019 and 3,000, respectively. This was hardly surprisingly, though, bearing in mind the scale of the devastation and deportation which the inhabitants had experienced during the war years. For the total population had fallen from 1,200,000 at its outbreak to only 341,000 by late 1944.[16] To this end, the Soviet Jewish Solomon Michoels attempted to foster a plan for Crimea to become a Jewish republic. However, Stalin, who had now entered his most anti-semitic phase, rejected this proposal. Nonetheless, a few thousand Ashkenazi Jews did indeed return and by 1959 no less than 26,000 Jews had settled in Crimea.[17] Ethnic Russians also flocked there and by the late 1950s the population had returned to its pre-war levels, in excess of a million. The majority were now Russians (71.4 per cent), the largest minority Ukrainians (22.3 per cent).[18] More than 80,000 dwellings expropriated from the Tatars were provided to accommodate them, along with land and half a million head of livestock.[19] Crimea had come to possess an overwhelmingly Russian cultural and ethnic identity, one which it would maintain to this day.

TRANSFERRAL OF CRIMEA TO UKRAINE AND ITS PLACE IN THE POST-SOVIET PERIOD

Transfer of Crimea to Ukraine

During the 1950s, first under Stalin and then under Nikita Khrushchev (1894–1971) Crimea and its people had virtually no say in its destiny. Khrushchev transferred Crimea to Ukraine in 1954, to celebrate the tricentennial of the union of Ukraine with Russia. At least, this has been the received view, in order to celebrate the 200th anniversary of the annexation of Ukraine to Russia.[1] However, the personal role of Khruschev is a widely disputed issue amongst many historians, especially Russian ones, as most discussions of the Communist Party of the Soviet Union's governing bodies were not recorded. In 1953–55 (Georgy) Malenkov (briefly head as First Secretary of the CPSU from September 1953 and also Chairman of the Council of Ministers from 1953–55) was treated as leader of the country, as can be seen by the order of precedence of party personages recorded in Soviet newspapers at that time. In any case, it was only after his fall in February 1955, that Khruschev can be said to have become the undisputed leader. Be that as it may, the legality of the transfer according to the Soviet laws in place in 1954 also continues as a matter of dispute. In part this was done as a public relations exercise, intended to some degree to lend him the image of a Ukrainian patriot and to obliterate the notoriety in the public consciousness of his policies which encouraged the death by famine of millions of Ukrainian peasants who were obstinate in their rejection of Communism. It was also done as a way of keeping the immediate responsibility for Crimea at arm's length from Moscow, enabling the peninsula to serve as a testing ground for a new initiative to further industrialise it, with workers provided from Russia, many from Voronezh.

This was followed in 1956–57 by the rehabilitation of many Tatars deported from Crimea during the Second World War, part of the wider rehabilitation of numerous non-Russian ethnic peoples who had been deported during the Stalin era. However, unlike the Chechens, Ingush and others, whose ancestral homelands were in the Caucasus, the Crimean Tatars were not invited to return home. Indeed, it was only in 1968, that the Tatar Crimeans dared to submit petitions to the authorities, said to contain some three million signatures requesting the right to return. However, these requests continued to fall on deaf ears for another generation. So, according to the first post-war census of 1959, Crimea had become and continued to remain an almost thoroughly Slavic state – 93 per cent out of a total of 1.2 million (71 per cent Russian, 22 per cent Ukrainian at this time).[2] Its political identity and destiny was now subsumed into that of the highly centralised Soviet Union, whose fate it shared with little heed to the needs of its local population during the Cold War period.

Industrial Development

The further development of heavy industry was of primary importance to the Soviet authorities during the decades following the Second World War. One major focus for this redevelopment was the iron ore complex in the environs of Kerch which had been devastated during the war. This endeavour proved so successful that by 1975 was attaining thirty-nine times its pre-war production levels.[3] The chemical industry was also expanded to an extraordinary degree, in particular, the Armyansk complex which processed salt from the Sivash Sea and Crimean lakes of the northern steppes. All this was facilitated by the construction of the North Crimean Canal (built from 1963–1975), which connected the Dnieper River to the environs of Kerch, with two subsidiary branches extending outwards towards Yevpatoria. Where there was work there was also population growth. Thus, the Crimean population continued to expand so that by 1989, the population had reached well over two million, including 1.6 million Russians and 626,000 Ukrainians. During this Soviet post-war period, Sevastopol maintained a special status because of its highly important naval base over which Moscow exercised direct administrative control. It, too, thrived, as did the Crimean capital itself Simferopol, which by the 1980s boasted in excess of 300,000 inhabitants.[4]

Agriculture and Food Processing

Along with heavy industry, some sectors of agriculture were resurrected and massively developed. This was especially true of viniculture which now catered for a mass market. The dessert wines of Massandra and Crimean sparkling wine became popular throughout the Soviet Union and its satellite states. These were not the elegant wines of the imperial and interwar period but sweet wines which appealed to the less jaded palettes of those not previously used to such luxuries. Between the beginning of the post-war period and 1979 the amount of land planted with vines was increased seven-fold in order to meet the demand. Fruits and nuts were also cultivated, along with essential oils like lavender and rose, and herbs such as sage. This meant that 44 per cent of Crimea's total production was now devoted to food processing. Other crops, however, in particular, cotton, were abandoned.[5]

Health Spa and Primary Tourist Destination of the Soviet Union

Already during the later imperial days, the benefits of Crimea's coastal climate throughout the year had been widely appreciated. But it was only in the postwar decades that this aspect of Crimea was significantly developed. By the 1970s, there were some 105 sanatoria, along with twenty-four rest homes, which accommodated no less than 46,000 patients. Additional to these, a plethora of hotels were constructed, with the capacity for up to 80,000 visitors at any one time in the summer, and even in the winter attracting over 40,000 Soviet travellers for whom visits to warmer climes were virtually impossible because of limitations on foreign travel.[6] Thus, up to four million people from all over the Soviet Union came to Crimea each year. These included not only factory workers and members of the military, but the country's rulers themselves: Stalin visited Koreyiz, Brezhnev went to Oreanda and Gorbachev to Foros, although each also had the option of staying in similarly balmy Sochi. Crimea now had what was, for a Communist country, a highly developed infrastructure: the country's first mountain trolley-bus line opened in 1961 to passengers wishing to connect from the rail and air terminal at Simferopol to the coastal resorts.[7]

Gradual Rehabilitation of the Crimean Tatars

The Crimean Tatars, some of whom were tainted by wartime collaboration with the Germans, found that it took decades for their rehabilitation to be completed. During the early post-war years until the death of Stalin, they were not only forbidden from returning to Crimea, but also suffered many constraints on their movements even within the central Asian regions of the Soviet Union to which they had been deported. A first step towards their rehabilitation occurred when, in 1954–56 under Khrushchev, some of these constraints were lifted. A decade later, a symbolic improvement took place, when on 5 September 1967 they were absolved as a collective people from the crime of collaboration. This action, however, did not result in the right to return to their native land. Nonetheless, some Tatars began to enjoy a de facto, if not de jure, improvement in their lot and no less than 10,000 Tatars were emboldened enough in 1967–68, to up stakes in Uzbekistan and migrate back to Crimea, despite the formal prohibition from making such a move. The majority were forced to return or to move elsewhere, but some 900 families did successfully re-establish themselves in their homeland in 1968–69. By now, a campaign was underway which included not only Crimean Tatars but Ukrainian dissidents who supported them, such as Petro Grigorenko, Sviatoslav Karavansky, and Viacheslav Chornovil. Its course, however, did not run smoothly and, in 1978, a Crimean Tatar Musta Mamut immolated himself, taking inspiration from Buddhist monks who had carried out similar auto-da-fé in Vietnam during the war with the United States a few years before.

The situation for Crimean Tatars changed dramatically, though, in the atmosphere of *perestroika* which was implemented under Gorbachev. When a Tatar demonstration took place in Red Square, in July 1987, it proceeded with few constraints. Indeed, the Soviet government established a commission to respond to their complaints. The end result of this was a decree in November 1989 – at a point when only about 20,000 Crimean Tatars resided in Crimea – which granted them the right to return to their ancestral homeland. Within only seven months no fewer than 135,000 Crimean Tatars had availed themselves of this right.[8]

Re-establishment of Crimean Autonomy

In 1991 Crimea was permitted to re-establish a modicum of autonomy through the re-establishment of the Crimean Soviet Socialist Republic, a constituent republic within the Soviet Union, a choice voted for by no less than 93 per cent of the electorate in a referendum.[9] However, this arrangement proved short lived. Ukraine, which had declared itself independent only half a year before, overruled this decision by declaring Crimea an autonomous republic within the wider Ukrainian Soviet state in February 1991. This decision from on high would have ominous consequences for the future, failing, as it did, to take any cognisance of the wishes of its people. At the time, President Yeltsin, preoccupied with so many other issues, had no great desire to re-annex Crimea.

A third political force also vied for Crimean domination. It was that of the Mejlis, the administrative body of the recently returned Crimean Tatars, who wished to create another Tatar republic along the lines of Tatarstan (embedded in the heartland of Russia between Moscow and the Urals, the capital of which was Kazan). but devoid of a Soviet link. Rather they wished Crimea to become a state in which the three 'indigenous' peoples of Crimea – the Crimean Tatars, Krymchaks and Karaites – could have a dominating role. Its leader was Mustafa Dzhemilev (b. 1943), a long-time Soviet dissident and sometime inmate of the Gulag. Unfortunately for these aspirations, other peoples, including Slavs and Armenians also saw themselves as part of the ancient population of Crimea, some having ancestors who had resided longer in Crimea than those of the Tatars. Thus, the Tatars were not recognised internally or internationally as the 'indigenous' inhabitants of Crimea.

In the end, in September 1991, the Parliament of Crimea claimed for itself the sovereignty of Crimea. Whilst it disputed the legitimacy of 'Khrushchev's gift' of Crimea to Soviet Ukraine, it nonetheless acquiesced in allowing the republic to be subsumed within the new independent Ukrainian state, seeing no viable alternative at the time. The following year the promulgation by the Crimean parliament of a new constitution was enacted, which was soon succeeded by a second one. According to this one, Russian, Crimean Tatar and several other historic languages in use in Crimea were all granted official protection with respect to public usage, with Ukrainian, nonetheless, confirmed as the principal official language. The subsuming of Crimea within the wider state of Ukraine was thus accomplished. However, many pro-Russians took exception to this and gave their support to Yury Meshkov (b. 1945) as president of the Autonomous Republic of Crimea. Many Tatars, in turn, still smarting from their decades of deportation, rejected this and turned to Ukraine instead. This pro-Ukrainian stance became the official policy of the Mejlis and its leader Mustafa Dzhemilev.

Meanwhile, back in Kiev, the Ukrainian government took an increasingly tough line with respect to Crimea, which culminated, in 1995, in the abolition of not only the office of Crimean president but the validity of any Crimean constitutions. Political authority over Crimea was now, by its own unilateral decision, invested in the Ukrainian government in Kiev, meaning that rule over Crimea was henceforth invested in an independent Ukraine's second president, Leonid Kuchma (b. 1938).

Special Status of Sevastopol

During the Soviet period, the naval base and other military installations in and around Sevastopol had enjoyed immense significance, not least during the Cuban Missile Crisis of October-November 1962. The secret placing of Soviet ballistic missiles in Castro's Cuba had been uncovered by the United States military, leading to a naval blockade and confrontation between the two superpowers and led the world to the brink of nuclear catastrophe. Elements in the negotiations involved the removal of NATO missiles from Turkey, just across the Black Sea from Crimea, and although they have since been shown to have been obsolete at the time, their removal under a secret treaty by the United States, had been important in resolving the issue, along with the removal of the Soviet Missiles from Cuba.[10] Thereafter, Sevastopol remained of crucial importance, symbolically and in practice, for Russia's naval presence in the Mediterranean world.

Thus, it was of the utmost importance for Russia that in the post-Soviet period the special status of Sevastopol, Inkerman and Balaklava (along with a few interior sites) was reconfirmed. This action, however, cut these places off from local Crimean administrative influence, giving the reigns of power over them instead to the Kiev government itself. Yet this was an extraordinary political anomaly since Sevastopol was and continued to be the home of Russia's Black Sea Fleet, which, in 1995, had some 300 combat ships stationed there, along with fourteen submarines. There were also no fewer than 300 aeroplanes and helicopters, serviced by more than 35,000 airmen and other ancillary personnel.[11] Two years later, in May 1997, as a way of resolving this conundrum, Russia and Ukraine signed their Friendship Treaty which provided Russia with a lease over Sevastopol until 2017. This was a protocol which merely delayed catastrophe in the wider region for the next generation. But at the time it granted Russia, under a leasehold agreement, the right to maintain 80 per cent of its fleet in Crimea, an arrangement that in 2010 was renewed until 2042, by the now, from both sides, discredited pro-Russian fourth president of Ukraine, Viktor Yanukovich (b. 1950).

Tatar Life in Post-Soviet Crimea

During this post-Soviet period, the Crimean Tatar population had not only successfully re-established itself but grown, according to the census of 2001, to more than 243,000 (some sources place it as high as 300,000), that is, at least 12 per cent of the total population of Crimea, a remarkable comeback over a period of less than a generation.[12] However, many of these Crimean Tatars were amongst the poorest and least educated of the inhabitants of Crimea, living in primitive makeshift dwellings on the outskirts of Simferopol and other urban areas. Crimea suffered a dearth of affordable housing for almost all ethnic communities and this was particularly so for those who were Crimean Tatar and who had returned to their homeland with virtually nothing. To alleviate this problem, the United Nations granted some 15 million dollars as part of its Crimea Integration and Development Programme, established in 1994.[13] However, this initiative failed to dramatically ameliorate the situation, since poverty and unemployment – up to a third of Crimean men were unemployed, the highest rate of any ethnic community in the region – continued to plague the Tatar community. In consequence, by the end of the millennium, almost half the Crimean Tatar population still subsisted in makeshift housing.[14] As for the Ukrainian government in Kiev, its focus was now on other more pressing economic issues increasingly afflicting areas within Ukraine which were seen as more important to Kiev than Crimea.

Local initiatives were undertaken to improve the material and cultural well-being of the Crimean Tatars. The Gaspirali Crimean Tatar National Library, for example, was opened again at Simferopol, in 1990, and took on a role of international significance in the preservation of Tatar literary culture. Tatar education was now encouraged, albeit in a limited way, with thirteen schools providing a basic education for 4,000 pupils through the medium of the Crimean Tatar language, a major innovation.[15] International contributors also came to play an increasingly important role, not least Turkey, which provided several million dollars to the General Centre of Crimean Tatar Associations, as well as the Crimea Foundation.[16] This occurred against a wider political and economic backdrop, with Turkish industries and companies, particularly in construction, playing an ever more important role in the economy of both Ukraine and Russia.

On a political level, matters also seemed to be improving. From 1994–98, Crimean Tatars occupied fourteen seats in parliament, in Simferopol. However, changes which were introduced into the electoral system supporting single candidate mandates in 1998, soon decreased their presence, as did the introduction in 2006 of yet another new electoral system based on proportional representation. Now the Crimean Tatars had to be content with a more vociferous and politically powerful Slavic majority.

Re-establishment of the Armenian Community

As the collapse of the Soviet Union unfolded in the late 1980s, the Armenian community of Crimea enjoyed a revival. In 1989, the Armenian Luys (Light) Society was founded, renamed the Crimean Armenian Society in 1996 and composed of four branches. Run by the National Council of Crimean Armenians, the higher administration of which is invested in its National Congress, it has been meeting at least every four years and taking an increasingly pro-Russian stance. Amongst its activities are responsibilities for managing the Luys Cultural and Ethnographic Centre, at Surb-Khach in Stary Krym. It has also published *Dove Masis*, a monthly newspaper and has supported Armenian television and radio broadcasts. The former includes the twice monthly Armenian language programme Barev and five weekly radio broadcasts. With the Armenian Apostolic Church enjoying a good relationship with the Russian Orthodox Church, to which most inhabitants of Crimea belong, the Armenian churches reopened in Yalta, Feodosia and Yevpatoria and a new secondary school was established in Simferopol in 1998. As of 2003, the Armenian population had increased to at least 20,000, most of them living in the above-mentioned cities, as well as in Kerch, Sevastopol and Sudak,[17] although there are said to be only 557 Armenians now living in the environs of Feodosia, a city which was formerly the *hochburg* of Armenian life in Crimea.[18]

Restoration of Historic Monuments in the Post-Soviet Period

It was an irony that many historic edifices which had survived the Great War, Revolution, Civil War and Second World War came to be destroyed by neglect towards the end of the Soviet period. The Naryshkin Mansion was one such example. Whilst the Salgirka Park and gardens, in which it was situated, were maintained and improved for agricultural purposes, having been transferred in 1966 to the Simferopol Pedagogical Institute (renamed the Simferopol State University in 1972), the house, now given over to shops, was not. Then in 1985 a fire severely damaged the structure. Work on the reconstruction of the Naryshkin Mansion was finally started in 1992. With its transfer to the ownership of the Ukrainian National Academy of Sciences and Ministry of Education and Science, a sympathetic series of restorations were finally carried out.

Another building to undergo major restoration and renovation was St Vladimir's Cathedral, which had been ruined once again during the Second World War (it was originally built in the neo-Byzantine style between 1850–1876) and was reconstructed between 1997–2001, at Chersonesus, near Sevastopol. The principal architect of this reconstruction was E. Osadchiy. Both Putin, newly chosen president of Russia, and Leonid Kuchma, acted as the principal patrons of the endeavour, so rich in spiritual and historical symbolism was St Vladimir's. A number of monasteries were also rebuilt, including the Formation Monastery near Bakhchisaray and the

Inkermann Monastery, near Sevastopol, as the Russian Orthodox revival permeated ever wider.

New monuments commemorating the past have also been funded. Thus, a large monument in Kerch, crowned by a Russian Orthodox Cross, was erected, commemorating those Russians, in general, and Crimeans, in particular, who were murdered by the Reds during the Revolution of 1917 and in the ensuing Civil War.

Russian-Western Tug of War

From the start of the post-Soviet period, Crimea increasingly became the object of a tug of war between Russia and the West. It also occasionally enjoyed the attention of the world, not least in economic terms. During the honeymoon days after Ukraine declared itself independent and began to take a more western cause, it benefited from international funds. These favoured not only Crimean Tatars but also other non-Russian minority groups such as the Karaites. Thus, the Karaite district of Yevpatoria underwent a major restoration, in particular, its Kenesa which was decorated with Hebrew liturgical script and reconsecrated in 2005, when the International Karaite Festival was held in Yevapatoria.

Within Ukraine, however, and despite its autonomy, Crimea was considered by the authorities in Kiev as a region apart, Russian looking and whose leading historical cultural figures, like Pushkin and Chekhov, were associated with Russia, rather than Ukraine. In consequence, many connected with Crimea, both native and foreign, began to see Crimea as the Cinderella of the Ukrainian state, especially, in financial terms, when Ukrainian resources were limited and therefore went to the heartland rather than the periphery.

There were also political issues increasingly entering the equation. The Ukrainian Foreign Minister Volodymyr Ohryzko took vociferous exception to Russia in September 2008 for granting Russian passports to Crimeans desirous of acquiring them. This occurred against a backdrop of growing economic crisis in Ukraine, in part the result of the world wide economic crisis which had recently erupted but in part because of the debilitating economic corruption which had completely sapped the Ukrainian economy. Ever increasing numbers of people in Crimea began to look on Russia as the solution to their problems, since the Russian economy seemed to be thriving as never before, because of its booming oil and gas industries. Yet if Crimea and much of the east of Ukraine looked to Russia, the west of the country and pockets elsewhere throughout looked increasingly to Europe, its crisis notwithstanding, because of its more stable infrastructure and economic and political transparency. This would eventually lead in late 2013 to what in Crimea was known as Euromaidan, in Kiev, to some a rightwing nationalist coup, to others a liberal revolution.

EPILOGUE:
CRIMEA IN THE TWENTY-FIRST CENTURY

The Dawn of the New Millennium

By the beginning of the twenty-first century, the population of Crimea was just under two million, a modest decline from the previous census of a decade before but one which, nonetheless showed a relatively thriving region of some industry and tourism which attracted visitors from both mainland Ukraine and Russia. In 2001, Russians made up the majority of those living in the Crimea, but Ukrainians also made up a quarter of the population and there were sizeable communities of other national and ethnic groups. These included Crimean Tatars (12.1 per cent), as well as Belarusians, and smaller minorities of other Tatar ethnicities, as well as Greeks, Armenians, Jews, Germans, Bulgarians, Poles, Azerbaijanis, Gypsies and even Koreans. Most of the inhabitants, including the Tatars, spoke, indeed, still speak, Russian as their mother tongue. Sizeable numbers of students from Russian academic institutions also regularly visited, staying at special accommodation which had since Soviet, even imperial, days been provided for that purpose.

There was also a sizeable development of food industries, vineyards and other such activities in the agriculture sector. Amongst the most important, though, was tourism, since Crimea boasted wonderful weather for most of the year, stunning national parks of international ecological importance and beautiful palaces, churches and monasteries, along with battlefields of great significance. The health industry, based around numerous spas and sanitoria, also attracted thousands of visitors from both Russia and Ukraine. Of course, political and military upheavals in the nearby Caucasus, in Chechnya, Georgia, South Ossetia and Abkhazia, had their negative implications for Crimea's union with Ukraine, since, at the time of the collapse of the Soviet Union, the majority of the inhabitants saw Russia, rather than Ukraine, as their motherland. This state of affairs was hardly surprising since many people had migrated to Crimea from Russia in recent decades. Moreover, the fact that there was a continued Russian naval presence within Ukraine, many of whose citizens were keen to expel it before the lease was expected to run out in 2017, also created problems. Some of these Ukrainians looked towards NATO and the European Union for their future prosperity, whilst many of the pro-Russian citizens of Crimea perceived NATO and the European Union as aggressively expansionist and therefore hostile. In consequence, anti-NATO protests broke out in Feodosia in 2006. This was but the latest in an old but deepening east-west fault line running not only through Crimea, but also Ukraine and its largest cities, Kiev and Odessa. This was reflected not only in the spheres of politics and economics, but in religion as well, for by now there were no less than one canonical Ukrainian Orthodox Church under the Patriarch of Moscow, and two non-canonical under competing Ukrainian patriarchs, not recognised by other canonical Orthodox churches. Additionally, there were both Latin and Greek Rite Catholic Churches. The latter tended to be pro-European in their stances, but the canonical Ukrainian Orthodox Church, with the largest number of adherents in Ukraine, was decidedly pro-Russian. On my first visit to Crimea in 2006, even a foreigner such as I could, therefore, see that storm clouds loomed on the horizon and it was already then that I felt that the need for a book on the history of Crimea seemed necessary to facilitate an understanding of the peninsula and the implications for the future.

When, in April 2008, the Russian Society of Crimea celebrated the 225th Anniversary of Catherine the Great's Crimean Manifesto of 1783, annexing Crimea to Russia, it became even clearer that many in Crimea were not happy with the political status quo. Then, in December 2009, the United Russian Party staged a pro-Russian demonstration, accompanied by images of Zaporozhian Cossack Hetman Bogdan Khelminsky who had successfully fought against the Polish-Lithuanian Commonwealth in the seventeenth century and thereafter accepted the suzerainty of Russia.

Few, however, realised the degree to which violence would break out only a few years later after President Viktor Yanukovych regained the reigns of power in Ukraine. Now the country was on the brink of a catastrophic fratricidal war, in which the majority of combatants on both sides had

Russian as well as Ukrainian ancestry. In part, this was a result of the rise of the Ukrainian nationalistic political right, a small minority to be sure but a vociferous one. By May 2013, both the United Russia Party and the Russian Society of Crimea were already actively demonstrating and campaigning against what they perceived as the growing power of this Ukrainian far right, some of whose members many pro-Russians associated with the Ukrainian Nazi leader Stepan Bandera, notorious from the Second World War, known in Russia as the 'Great Patriotic War'. That said, it was the events of Maidan Square in December 2013, which really wrought dramatic changes to the public consciousness in Crimea.

In January 2014, massive demonstrations by both the United Russia Party and the Russian Society of Crimea again took place, though these were now directed specifically against not only 'Euromaidan', as the Russian speakers called the events of Maidan, but NATO and the European Union, who were felt to have contributed to the uprisings in Kiev and what was perceived as a coup overthrowing Yanukovych. Some of these took place outside the High Council of Crimea, in the capital Simferopol. In early February, these were countered by pro-European demonstrations, which in turn provoked even larger pro-Russian ones. Towards the end of the month a commemorative march was held, remembering those who had died at Maidan, led by pro-Russian activists Sergey Aksenov and D. Polonsky. Shortly thereafter, Aksenov and others met up with deputies of the Russian Duma, with a view to enabling the reunion of Crimea to Russia. The following day, a great assembly was held at the High Council. This included not only members of the United Russia Party, under M. Sheremet, and the Russian Society of Crimea but pro-Ukrainian factions, even including the Tatar Medjlis Council and the extreme Right Sector faction, some of whom wore balaclavas during public demonstrations outside. By contrast to the violent events in Kiev, however, deadly violence was avoided. Aksenov was now widely accepted by most Crimeans as their leader and was proclaimed prime minister. This government also included a variety of pro-Russian members, including L. Opanasyuk, K. Bacharev, G. Ioffe, P. Temirgaliev, O. Kovitidi and D. Dolonskiy. For most of the pro-Russian inhabitants of Crimea, the majority of its people, this was the fruit of what they now termed their 'Crimean Spring.' For Ukraine, of course, and its anti-Russian government the view was quite the opposite. For them, Crimea was being illicitly annexed by Russia, against the will of the people of Ukraine.

Operation Polite People

Russian Minister of Defence General Sergey Kuzhugetovich Shoygu (b. 1955) famously dubbed those men in green uniform who had, according to the Russian view, come to defend Crimea, as 'polite people' (the hostile Kiev government called them 'Little Green Men' because of their olive green uniforms), possibly up to 20,000 men, some of whom were in elite *spetznaz* units. Their purpose was to preserve order by securing Russian military bases and other important buildings and to prevent the newly established western-orientated government in Kiev, from which many in Crimea felt alienated, from making inroads in Crimea or fomenting violence there.

General Valery Gerasimov (b. 1955), Chief of the Russian General Staff, was the author of the new style so-called hybrid war which now came to be waged to the north of Crimea, in eastern Ukraine, and which would have major implications for the peninsula. This type of war is based on the use of special forces, the identity of whom are shadowy, rather than conventional soldiers, which, through a mixture of nondescript commando actions, propaganda and other non-conventional hostile activities, now play a major role in international strife in many parts of the world on all sides. Moscow born Igor Vsevolodovich Girkin (b. 1970), also known as Igor Strelkov, has been one key figure in this military activity, leading the Donetsk insurgency against the Ukrainian authorities, established in Kiev after the fall of Yanukovych. Said to be motivated by the old fashioned, cherished Russian values of autocracy, the Church and the nation (as was first articulated by the Minister of Education Sergey Uvarov, as far back as 1833), his ideology finds considerable resonance throughout Russia and in the Kremlin even today. A colonel in the FSB, Strelkov has since left the region, returning to Moscow, but it has become clear through him that pro-Russian insurgents themselves vary in their goals and values. Indeed, the murder of two FSB officers killed in Donetsk by pro-Russian rebels demonstrates that President Putin is in no way the deus ex machina of the revolt from Ukrainian rule, but merely one component in the complex arena of pro-Russia activists and the principal defender of Russian identity and interests in the region. This became clear when Lugansk commander Alexander Bednov ('Batman') was murdered in late December 2014 by other militants. Some have maintained that the FSB themselves were obliged to take violent action to ensure the submission of the movement's more unruly members. Be that as it may, there is no doubt that military and insurgent activity in the east of Ukraine exerts considerable pressures on Crimea and its northern land border. Moreover, with Ukraine blocking the transport of many goods and services over the Perekop Peninsula and with the Straits of Kerch frequently disrupting these by sea, through storms and other logistical difficulties, coastal cities in eastern Ukraine, like Mariupol, assume a new strategic importance. To what degree Russia will find it a necessity to secure through this city Crimea's lifeblood supply of water and gas for the future, remains to be seen but in early 2015 it briefly came under attack by pro-Russia activists, with considerable loss of civilian life. Until chronic transport and supply problems are resolved, Crimea will not be able to consolidate and develop its economic and social infrastructure. Not military activity, but negotiation on a multitude of levels will provide the ultimate and only resolution of the crisis with respect to both Crimea and Ukraine. Either people come to thrive on both sides of the new border or both suffer – that is the bleak but inevitable conclusion which history teaches those who study it.

Union with Russia and its Aftermath

A Russian-held referendum on 16 March 2014 declared that most Crimeans wanted the autonomous republic, together with separately administered Sevastopol, to join the Russian Federation; the Russian government acceded to this 'request' and Crimea became a part of the Russian Federation, wide-spread international disapproval notwithstanding. President Putin presided over this 'happy reunion of Crimea to Russia', which, though utterly condemned by the new Kiev government, United States and European Union, was joyfully received by most Crimeans. Observers from some twenty-one countries were said to have witnessed the referendum, including Tatyana Zhdanok, an ethnic Russian from Latvia who is a member of the European Parliament, although many sceptical western observers who would have liked to have been there were excluded. Nonetheless, the renowned American non-partisan American Pew Research Centre, based in Washington, confirmed that at least 54 per cent of Crimeans support the reunion to Russia.[1] The following month, on 11 April 2014, the new Crimean government promulgated a new Crimean constitution, which confirmed its reunion with Russia.

The choice given had been between reunion with Russia, as a constituent republic of the Russian Federation or for the restoration of the constitution of the Republic of Crimea of 1992, within Ukraine. According to Russian statistics, 96.77 per cent of the 2.4 million inhabitants voted to join Russia. Many western governments and Ukrainian supporters of the new government in Kiev considered the referendum a travesty. Throughout much of Crimea, though, there was jubilation but not everywhere, least amongst the Crimean Tatars and those who had come from the mainland of Ukraine. Some, even amongst those who supported the union, considered that it had been carried out with unseemly haste. Others, however, felt that due to the volatile situation in Kiev and elsewhere in Ukraine rapid and decisive action was required in order to stabilise the situation in Crimea and to avoid bloodshed.

Figures who had long played a prominent role in Crimean political life now came to the fore. One such was Olga Kovitidi (b. 1962), a Crimean of Greek extraction from Simferopol, who was appointed vice-chairman of the Crimea Council of Ministers in February 2014. She also now serves as the republic's representative on the Russian Federation Council in Moscow. Trained as a lawyer in Odessa, Kovitidi had become deputy of the State Council of Crimea in 2006. Vice-speaker Sergey Tsekov had already previously been appointed to the Council. The highest political position in Crimea, though, went to Sergey Aksenov (b. 1972), who was appointed acting governor, in April. As for Sevastopol, former Vice-admiral of the Black Sea Fleet, Sergey Menyaylo, was put in charge.

The Tatars in the Wake of the Annexation of Crimea to Russia

Many Tatars, although by no means all, disapproved of what they perceived as Russia's annexation of their homeland. Having suffered enormous hardships during the Soviet period, it was only to be expected that many Tatars preferred to disassociate themselves from Russia. This, of course, did not go unnoticed in the Kremlin and so, the Crimean Tatar leader Mustafa Dzhemilev, outspoken in his opposition, became a target for Russian hostility. Kovitidi personally commented on his ban of entrance, delivered at the border in April, justifying it by the increased political instability it would cause, were he allowed to return. This led to his exclusion from Russia as a whole and Crimea in particular, until 2019. Some in the west saw him as bulwark of that small minority in Crimea who rejected what they perceived to be Russia's annexation and so came to his public defence. As a symbolic gesture of support for both him and the Tatar peoples of Crimea, Dzhemilev was granted the Lech Walesa Solidarity Prize in June 2014. Yet not all Tatars rejected union and some, like pro-Russian Lenur Islyamov, even took an active part in the new Crimean council. A leading Crimean Tatar business magnate and philanthropist, he was the founder of Crimea's first Tatar television channel, ATR. A descendant of deportees and with, at the time, a daughter studying in Britain and two sons in Russia, he straddled both sides of the international and internal divide. His film *Khaitarma* (2013) about the deportations of 1944 won him both international fame, as well as notoriety, the latter, in particular, amongst those who resented his negative attitudes towards the Soviet system. However, on 28 May, Islyamov was dismissed as acting deputy prime minister. Ruslan Balbek, another Crimean Tatar, but hostile to the Mejlis (Tatar Parliament) took his place. This led Refat Chubarov, head of the Mejlis, to condemn this new appointment.

Implementation of Sanctions

All this instability and uncertainty in Crimea was further aggravated by the western introduction of sanctions, first advocated by United States President Barack Obama. Numerous western investors in the peninsula were horrified and spoke out against them but their warnings have not been heeded. Indeed, towards the end of December 2014, matters worsened when both MasterCard and Visa, under political pressure, suspended their acceptance of the use of their credit cards in Crimea, curtailing tourism even further than had already been the case. Paypal suspended its online secure payment system, as did Google its Ad Sense online advertising department. Later in January 2015, eBay suspended its activities in and with Crimea.

NATO and Crimea

NATO's attitude to Crimea over the last year seems to have been one of confusion, in failing to take account of the peninsula's historical context, ethnic make up and popular will. There is no doubt that the majority of the population of Crimea supports joining the Russian Federation. Indeed, during its post-Soviet years, under Ukrainian sovereignty, it had become, in the opinion of many, something of a burden, its status as an autonomous republic seen more as a liability than a benefit for Ukraine, because it continually drained from the heartland of Ukraine. For that reason, financial resources were more reluctantly sent to Crimea by Kiev than to elsewhere in Ukraine, not least because of the profoundly Russian identity of much of its population.

The very different status and ethnic cum religious mix of the contested eastern edges of Ukraine around Donetsk form a very different scenario in political, military, economic and cultural terms but have become blurred together with that of Crimea. In fact, they are very different. In the west, little distinction is made in the media and, indeed, even by governments, between the two. A far more nuanced and clear sighted analysis to perceive why each is quite distinct must be carried out to satisfactorily define the problems with respect to both and to define them, before a successful resolution can be achieved.

Economic Difficulties

In the wake of the conflict with Ukraine and reunion with Russia, Crimea suffered serious economic difficulties. This was largely the result of the economic sanctions imposed on the autonomous republic by the United States and countries of the European Union, as well as a result of the closure of borders with Ukraine, which sharply reduced both imports and exports to Crimea. Tourism diminished sharply from about 5.9 million visitors in 2013 to only 3.3 million in 2014, and property values crashed. To remedy this in part, Russian offered some $12,000,000 for regional development over the next five years. Even the new Russian Minister for Crimean Affairs, Oleg Saveliev, admitted that times would get worse before they got better. The collapse of the rouble, now the currency of

Crimea instead of the Ukrainian hryvnia, to almost half its value further aggravated the situation. According to the Russian Federal Statistics Service, inflation had increased by almost a third by October 2014. Autumn storms and severe winter weather also wrought havoc, making the Straits of Kerch at times impassible and thereby hampering maritime trade from mainland Russia. How soon the projected nineteen-kilometre bridge over the straits will come to fruition – its cost could approach 5 billion dollars – remains to be seen. However, it should hardly be an insurmountable feat, bearing in mind that the Causeway Bridge over Lake Pontchartrain, in the American state of Louisiana, has been around for decades and is double the size, some thirty-eight kilometres in length. In any case, work on the bridge is now well underway.

Introduction of New Measures

Amongst the wide variety of new measures recently introduced in Crimea to improve the situation is the establishment of a free economic zone to make the peninsula more attractive. High technology companies are also being given incentives to come to Crimea, whilst air transport to and from Russia has doubled. New arrivals from Russia have more than filled the flight of Crimean residents who preferred to leave for mainland Ukraine. Russia is also providing at least some financial compensation to Crimeans whose savings were lost when Ukrainian banks shut down, removing their assets to the mainland with no compensation for those who had entrusted their savings to them.

On 15 August 2014, a further series of new measures was introduced at Yalta to ameliorate further the harsh economic realities. In the first instance, a long view was taken to develop Crimea as a destination for yachting, to make it, so to speak, a Russian Riviera. Henceforth, Russian yachting regulations would apply, an important change for the majority of yachts that visited the peninsula, in particular in the warmer months, many of which are foreign registered. In the wake of the reunion, the majority of yachts had, in any case, departed, so there was now a desperate need to woo them back. As of now they have not returned and the upper end of the tourist industry has in consequence declined dramatically. Only time will tell whether the new measures which are set to be introduced, subject to their acceptance by the Russian Ministry of Transport and other relevant bodies, improve the situation.

Softening of Sanctions on Crimea

On 30 January 2015, a softening of western sanctions with respect to Crimea could already be detected. The United States Department of the Treasury decided to permit, once again after the restrictions imposed on 19 December 2014, not only United States citizens but also Crimeans, not subject to specific sanctions, to receive funds in Crimea and to engage in other financial transactions of a non-commercial nature. Crimeans are also now permitted to maintain personal, non-business related, US bank accounts. A moratorium on the provision or maintenance of telecommunications equipment for any purpose was, however, continued. This and other actions are, however, not likely to reverse its union with Russia. It remains to be seen, though, to what degree Crimea will thrive under its return to Russian sovereignty, despite the continuing intractable hostility of the current Ukrainian government, and many western politicians and NATO. Certainly, the collapse of the electricity supply to Crimea in November 2015 – the result of the deliberate blowing up of the electricity pylons which were located north of Crimea's border – boded ill for future harmony, leaving, as it did, 1.6 million Crimean residents without power (this was eventually restored in December 2015). Widely labelled an act of terrorism, it led to the death of a rare white Bengal Tiger at Crimea's Yalta Zoo, just one of the many thousands of victims of the wider region's on-going military conflict. That said, Crimea has largely escaped the heavy losses seen in much of the Donetsk and Luhansk regions of eastern Ukraine, over 8,000 deaths according to the international press, with at most six people killed in Crimea in early 2014 and none since. It also remains to be seen how the theatre of war in Syria and Iraq, and the flow of refugees from these conflicted states, will exert any effects in Crimea. That said, Crimea has always come through the dreadful conflicts and natural disasters to which it has been subjected over the millennia remarkably well and so, in that sense, it seems likely that it will survive and thrive once again when this latest is laid to rest.

NOTES

CHAPTER 2 THE MIDDLE AGES

1   Magocsi, Paul Robert, *The Blessed Land: Crimea and the Crimean Tatars.* Toronto: Toronto University Press, 2014, p. 26.
2   Ascherson, Neal, *Black Sea: The Birthplace of Civilisation and Barbarism.* London: Vintage, 2007, p. 95.
3   Maksoudian, Krikor, 'Armenian Communities in Eastern Europe' in *Armenian People From Ancient to Modern Times, Volume II: Foreign Dominion to Statehood: The Fifteenth Century to the Twentieth Century*, Richard G. Hovannisian, (ed.). New York: St. Martin's Press, 1997, p. 54.

CHAPTER 3 THE CRIMEAN KHANATE AND OTTOMAN HEGEMONY

1   Królikowska, Natalia, 'Sovereignty and Subordination in Crimean-Ottoman Relations (Sixteenth-Eighteenth Centuries)' in *The European Tributary States of the Ottoman Empire in the Sixteenth and Seventeenth Centuries*, Gábor Kármán and Lovro Kunçević (eds.). Leiden/Boston: Brill, 2013, pp. 43-44.
2   Ivanics, Mária, 'The Military Co-operation of the Crimean Khanate with the Ottoman Empire in the Sixteenth and Seventeenth Centuries' in *The European Tributary States of the Ottoman Empire in the Sixteenth and Seventeenth Centuries*, Gábor Kármán and Lovro Kunçević (eds.). Leiden/Boston: Brill, 2013, pp. 275-278.
3   Özalp Gökbilgin (ed. and trans.) *Histoire de Sahip Giray, Khan de Crimée de 1532 à 1551.* Ankara, 1973, p. 114.
4   İnalcık, Halil, 'The Khan and the Tribal Aristocracy: The Crimean Khanate under Sahib Giray I' in *Harvard Ukrainian Studies,* 1979-80, 3-4, pp 45-451.

5   Rieber, Alfred J. *The Struggle for the Eurasian Borderlands: From the Rise of Early Modern Empires to the End of the First World War.* Cambridge: Cambridge University Press, 2014, p. 352.

6   Ivanics, pp. 279-280.

7   Królikowska, pp. 43-65.

8   Pamuk, Şevket, *A Monetary History of the Ottoman Empire,* Cambridge: Cambridge University Press, 2005, p. 105.

9   Acherson, Neal, *Black Sea: The Birthplace of Civilisation and Barbarism,* London: Vintage, 2007, p. 26.

10 Acherson, p. 243.

11 Ivanics, p. 281.

12 Penskoi, V.V. 'Voennyi potentsial Krymskogo Khanstva v konce XV-nachale XVII v.' *Vostok (Oriens)* [20], no. 2, 2010.

13 Ivanics, pp. 282-83

14 Ivanics, p. 294.

15 Ivanics, p. 284.

16 Królikowska, Natalia, Ibid., p. 53.

17 Ivanics, pp. 285-86.

18 Ivanics, pp. 296-297.

19 Ivanics, p. 297

20 Królikowska, p. 55.

21 Knolles, Richard, *The Generall Historie of the Turkes.* London: Adam Islip, 1603, p. 759.

22 Ivanics, p. 292.

23 Ivanics, p. 276.

24 Ivanics, p. 287.

25 Ivanics, pp. 289-290.

26 'Letter of Khan Gazi Giray II to the Polish King Sigismund III, 1592' in Kołodziejczyk, Dariusz, *The Crimean Khanate and Poland-Lithuania: International Diplomacy on the European Periphery (15th-18th Century): A Study of Peace Treaties Followed by Annotated Documents.* Leiden and Boston: Brill, 2011, document 34.

27 Ivanics, pp. 288-289.

28 Królikowska, p. 49.

29 Magocsi, Paul Robert, *The Blessed Land: Crimea and the Crimean Tatars.* Toronto: Toronto University Press, 2014, p. 49.

30 Ivanics, Mária, pp. 294-295.

31 Rieber, p.360.

32 Rieber, pp. 365-371.

CHAPTER 4 OTTOMAN ENCROACHMENT ON CRIMEA AND ITS RUSSIAN ANNEXATION

1   Ivanics, Mária, 'The Military Co-operation of the Crimean Khanate with the Ottoman Empire in the Sixteenth and Seventeenth Centuries' in *The European Tributary States of the Ottoman Empire in the Sixteenth and Seventeenth Centuries*, Gábor Kármán and Lovro Kunçević (eds.). Leiden/Boston: Brill, 2013, pp. 277-278.

2   Królikowska, Natalia, 'Sovereignty and Subordination in Crimean-Ottoman Relations (Sixteenth-Eighteenth Centuries)' in *The European Tributary States of the Ottoman Empire in the Sixteenth and Seventeenth Centuries*, Gábor Kármán and Lovro Kunçević (eds.). Leiden/Boston: Brill, 2013, p. 44.

3   Sebag Montefiore, Simon, *Prince of Princes:The Life of Potemkin,* London:Weidenfeld and Nicholson, 2000, p. 245.

4   Sebag Montefiore, p. 246.

5   Ibid.

6   Sebag Montefiore, p. 244.

7   Magocsi, Paul Robert, *The Blessed Land: Crimea and the Crimean Tatars.* Toronto: Toronto University Press, 2014, pp. 55-56.

8   Smiley, Will, '"After being so long Prisoners, they will not return to Slavery in Russia": An Aegean Network of Violence between Empires and Identities' in *Osmanlı Araştırmaları / The Journal of Ottoman Studies*, XLIV, 2014, p. 223.

9   Smiley, pp. 222 and 231.

10   Fisher, Alan, *The Crimean Tatars.* Stanford, CA.: Hoover Institution Press 1978, p. 78.

11   Figes, Orlando, *The Crimean War: A History.* New York: Picador, 2010, p. 20.

12   Figes, p. 21.

13   Magocsi, p. 59.

CHAPTER 5 THE CONSOLIDATION OF CRIMEA UNDER RUSSIAN CONTROL

1   Kozelsky, Mara, *Christianizing in the Russian Empire and Beyond.* De Kalb, IL.: Northern Illinois University Press, 2010, pp. 62-88.

2   Gleason, J., *The Genesis of Russophobia in Great Britain.* Cambridge, MA: Harvard University Press, 1950, p. 103.

3   FO 181/114, Palmerston to Ponsonby, 6 Dec. 1833.

4   Figes, Orlando, *The Crimean War: A History.* New York: Picador, 2010, p. 88.

5   Bitis, A., *Russia and the Eastern Question: Army, Government and Society 1815-1833.* Oxford: Oxford University Press, 2006, pp. 93-97.

6   Figes, pp. 67-70.

7   Fisher, Alan, *The Crimean Tatars*. Stanford, CA.: Hoover Institution Press 1978, p. 78.

CHAPTER 6 THE CRIMEAN WAR

1   Figes, Orlando, *The Crimean War: A History*. New York: Picador, 2010, pp. 2-3.

2   Foreign Office 78/413, Young to Palmerston, 29 Jan. and 28 Apr. 1840; 78/368, Young to Palmerston, 14 Mar. and 21 Oct. 1839, p. 5.

3   Figes, p. 9.

4   Chamberlain, M. *Lord Aberdeen: A Political Biography*, London: Longman, 1983, p. 476.

5   Figes, p.134.

6   Figes, p. 314.

7   Schroeder, P., Austria, *Great Britain and the Crimean War: The Destruction of the European Concert* (Ithaca, NY, p. 1972) pp. 193-4.

8   Kagan, Frederick W., *The Military Reforms of Nicholas I: The Origins of the Modern Russian Army*. London: Palgrave Macmillan, 1999, p. 243.

9   Figes, p. 144.

10   Benson, Arthur Christopher and Viscount Esher (eds.), *The Letters of Queen Victoria: A Selection from Her Majesty's Correspondence between the Years 1837 and 1861*, 3 vols. London: John Murray, 1907-8, vol. 2, p. 126.

11   Marline, R., 'L'Opinion franc-comtoise deviant la guerre de Crimeé' in *Annales Littéraires de l'Université de Besançon*, vol. 17. Paris, 1957, pp. 19-20.

12   Schiemann, T., *Geschichte Russlands unter Kaiser Nikolaus I*, 4 vols. Berlin, 1904-19, vol. 4, p. 430.

13   Figes, p. 160.

14   Tarle, E., *Krymskaia Voina*, vol. 1. Moscow, 1944, pp. 405-28.

15   Figes, pp. 13 and 16.

16   Maude, A., *The Life of Tolstoy: First Fifty Years*. London: Constable, 1908, pp. 96-7.

17   Zurrer, Werner (ed.), Akten zur Geschichte des Krimkriegs: Österreichische Akten zur Geschichte des Krimkriegs, ser. I, vol. 2. Munich, 1980, p. 248.

18   Kagan, p. 243.

19   Figes, p. 336.

20   de Damas, A., *Souvenirs Religieux et Militaires de la Crimée*. Paris: Jacques Lecoffre, 1857, pp. 147-8.

21   Figes, p. 228.

22   Baumgart, Winifried, *The Crimean War, 1853-1856*. London, Hodder Education, 1999, p. 116.

23 Hodasevich, R., *A Voice from within the Walls of Sebastopol: A Narrative of the Campaign in the Crimea and the Events of the Siege*. London: John Murray, 1856, p 35.

24 Figes, p. 206.

25 Masquelez, M., *Journal d'un Officier de Zouaves*. Paris, 1858, pp. 107-8.

26 Figes, p. 240.

27 Figes, p. 231.

28 Herbé, J., *Français et Russes en Crimée: Lettres d'un Officier Français à sa Famille pendant la Campagne d'Orient*. Paris, 1892, p. 337

29 Schroeder, P., *Austria, Great Britain and the Crimean War: The Destruction of the European Concert*. New York: Cornell University Press, 1972, pp. 204.

30 Figes, p. 272.

31 Figes, p. xvii.

32 Figes, p. 252.

33 Figes, pp. 268-69.

34 Cler, J., *Reminiscences of an Officer of Zouaves*. New York: D. Appleton, 1860, pp. 219-20.

35 Baron de Bazancourt, *The Crimean Expedition, to the Capture of Sebastopol*, 2 vols. London: Sampson Low, 1856, pp. 116-17.

36 Figes, p. 323.

37 Figes, p. 339.

38 Guerin, L., *Histoire de la Dernière Guerre de Russie (1853-1856)*, 2 vols. Paris: Dufour, Mulat, Boulanger, 1858, vol. 2, pp. 239-40.

39 Russell, William Howard, *The Times*, 28 May 1855.

40 Ibid.

41 Figes, pp. 352 and 396.

42 Verney, H., *Our Quarrel with Russia*. London, 1855, pp. 22-24.

43 Bayley, C., *Mercenaries for the Crimean: The German, Swiss, and Italian Legions in British Service 1854-6*. Montreal, 1977.

44 Figes, p.197.

45 Figes, p. 177.

46 Gordon, Charles George, *General Gordon's Letters from the Crimea, the Danube and Armenia*. London, 1884, p. 14.

47 Vitzthum von Eckstadt, K., *St Petersburg and London in the Years 1852-64*, 2 vols. London, 1887, vol I, p. 143.

48 St Aubyn, G., *Queen Victoria: A Portrait*. London: Atheneum Books 1991, p. 295.

49 Rappaport, H., *No Place for Ladies: The Untold Story of Women in the Crimean War*. London: Aurum Press, 2007, p. 77.

50 Figes, pp. 300-301.

51 Figes, p. 292.

52 Figes, p. 302.

53   Figes, pp. 303-04.

54   Tolstoy, Leo, *Sebastopol Sketches*, D. McDuff (trans.). London: Penguin, 1986, pp. 44, 47-48.

55   Figes, p. 253.

56   Figes, pp. 286-87.

57   Figes, p. 290.

58   Figes, pp. 48-49.

59   Figes, pp. 356-58.

60   Small, H., *The Crimean War: Queen Victoria's War with the Russian Tsars.* Stroud: The History Press, 2007, p.209.

61   Figes, p. 279.

62   Figes, pp. 381-85.

63   Russell, William Howard, *The Times*, 27 September 1855.

64   Figes, p. 395.

65   Figes, p. 397.

66   Margrave, R., 'Numbers & Losses in the Crimea: An Introduction' *War Correspondent*, 21/1 (2003) pp. 30-32; 21/2 (2003) pp.32-6; 21/3 (2003) pp. 18-22.

67   Murphy, David, *Ireland and the Crimean War.* Dublin: Four Courts Press, 2002, p. 104.

68   Hawthorne, N., *The English Notebooks, 1853-1856* (Columbus, OH: Ohio State University Press, 1997, p. 149.

69   Knollys, W., *The Victoria Cross in The Crimea: Deeds of Daring Library.* London: Dean & Son, 1877, p. vi.

CHAPTER 7 THE AFTERMATH OF THE CRIMEAN WAR

1   Hornby, Lady E., *Constantinople during the Crimean War.* London: Bentley, 1863, pp. 205-208.

2   Figes, Orlando, *The Crimean War: A History.* New York: Picador, 2010, p. 431.

3   *Lettre du Prince Moustapha Fazil à Sa Majesté Abdul Aziz, Sultan de Turquie, 1866.* Paris: Le Caire, 1940.

4   Kinross, Lord P., *Ottoman Centuries: The Rise and Fall of the Turkish Empire.* New York: Morrow Quill, 1977, p. 509.

5   Figes, p. 462.

6   Figes, pp. 421-22.

7   Williams, Brian Glyn, *The Crimean Tatars: The Diaspora Experience and the Forging of a Nation.* Leiden, Boston and Köln: Brill, 2001, p. 244.

8   Kozelsky, Mara, *Christianizing in the Russian Empire and Beyond.* De Kalb, IL.: Northern Illinois University Press, 2010, p.151.

9   Frank, J., *Dostoevsky: The Years of Ordeal, 1850-1859*. Princeton: Princeton University Press, 1983, p. 182.

10   Magocsi, Paul Robert, *The Blessed Land: Crimea and the Crimean Tatars*. Toronto: Toronto University Press, 2014, p. 65.

11   Magocsi, p. 105.

12   Magocsi, p. 107.

13   Best, Geoffrey, *Humanity in Warfare: The Modern History of the International Law of Armed Conflicts*. London: Routledge, 1980, p. 165.

14   Królikowska, Natalia, 'Sovereignty and Subordination in Crimean-Ottoman Relations (Sixteenth-Eighteenth Centuries)' in *The European Tributary States of the Ottoman Empire in the Sixteenth and Seventeenth Centuries*, Gábor Kármán and Lovro Kunçević (eds.). Leiden/Boston: Brill, 2013, p. 46.

15   Magocsi, pp. 72-73.

CHAPTER 8 FROM THE FIRST WORLD WAR TO SOVIET POWER

1   Magocsi, Paul Robert, *The Blessed Land: Crimea and the Crimean Tatars*. Toronto: Toronto University Press, 2014, p.82.

2   Bykova, Tetiana B., *Stvorennia Kryms'koi ASRR, 1917-1921*. Kiev: In-t istorii Ukrainy, 2011, p. 119.

3   Magocsi, p. 93

4   Magocsi, p. 95.

5   Magocsi, p. 95.

6   Magocsi, p. 98.

7   Magocsi, pp. 105-106.

8   Fisher, Alan, *The Crimean Tatars*. Stanford, CA.: Hoover Institution Press 1978, p. 141.

9   Lordkiparidze, R., (Head of the NKVD in Crimea), to the 18th Conference of the Coummunist Party of the Crimean A.S.S.R., Diulichev, Valerii *Krym: istoriia v ocherkakh-XX vet*. Simferopol, 2006, pp. 141-142.

10   http://www.ccssu.crimea.ua/crimea/etno/ethnos/armyane/index.htm

11   Magocsi, p. 105.

12   Diulichev, Valerii P., *Krym: istoriia v ocherkakh-XX vet*. Simferopol, 2006, p. 145.

13   Magocsi, p. 94.

14   Fisher, p. 142.

15   Magocsi, p. 103.

CHAPTER 9 THE SECOND WORLD WAR, YALTA, AND THE POST-WAR SETTLEMENT

1   Magocsi, Paul Robert, *The Blessed Land: Crimea and the Crimean Tatars.* Toronto: Toronto University Press, 2014, p. 117.

2   Roberts, Andrew, *The Storm of War. A New History of the Second World War.* London : Penguin, 2009, pp. 166-167.

3   Gerbet, Klaus (ed.), *von Bock, Generalfeldmarschall Fedor: War Diary 1939-1945.* Atglen, PA: Schiffer, 1996, pp. 289-90.

4   Magocsi, pp. 111-113.

5   Magocsi, p. 114.

6   Ibid.

7   Pohl, J. Otto, *Ethnic Cleansing in the USSR: 1937-1949*, from the series Contributions to the Study of World History, Number 65. Westport, CN: Greenwood Press, 1999, pp. 112-113.

8   Letter of A. Mokrousov and the secretary of the Simferopol Committee of the Communist party S. Martinov, dated July 1942, *Kozyts'kyi, Andrii Henotsyd ta polityka masovoho vynyshchennia tsyvil'noho naselennia u XX st.* L'viv, 2012, p. 366.

9   Valerii Diulichey, *Krym: istoria v ocherkakh-XXXX vek.* Simferopol, 2006, p. 236.

10 Sheehy, Anne 'The Crimean Tatars and Volga Germans: Soviet Treatment of Two National Minorities' in *Minority Rights Group Report*, No. 6. London, 1971, pp. 10-11.

11 Feodosia Office of Statistics.

12 Movsisyan, Jivan (24 June 1998), "Ղրիմահայոց ողբերգությունը" [The Tragedy of Crimean Armenians]. *Azg Daily* (in Armenian) (Yerevan).

13 Magocsi, p. 117.

14 Kozytskiy, Andriy, *Henotsyd ta polityka masovoho vynyshchennia tsyvil'noho naselennia u XX st.* Lviv, 2012, pp. 371-372.

15 Magocsi, p. 118.

16 Diulichev, Valeriy P., *Krym: istoria v ocherkakh-XX vek.* Simferopol, 2006, p. 196.

17 Magocsi, p. 106.

18 Chorniy, Serhiy, *Natsionalny skald naselennia Ukraïny v XX storichchy: dovidnyk.* Kiev, 2011, p. 76.

19 Kozytskiy, p. 370.

CHAPTER 10 TRANSFERRAL OF CRIMEA TO UKRAINE AND ITS PLACE IN THE POST-SOVIET PERIOD

1   Grigo Suny, Ronald *The Soviet Experiment: Russia, the USSR, and the Successor States.* New York: Oxford University Press, 1998, pp. 410-11.

2   Magocsi, Paul Robert, *The Blessed Land: Crimea and the Crimean Tatars.* Toronto: Toronto University Press, 2014, p. 118.

3   Diulichev, Valerii, *Krym: istoriya v ocherkakh-XX vet.* Simferopol, 2006, pp. 254-262.

4   Magocsi, p. 127.

5   Magocsi, p. 127.

6   *'Crimea' Encyclopedia of Ukraine,* Vol, I ed. Volodymyr Kubijovyč. Toronto, 1984, p. 617.

7   Magocsi, pp. 128-129.

8   Williams, Brian Glyn, *The Crimean Tatars: The Diaspora Experience and the Forging of a Nation.* Leiden, Boston, and Köln: Brill, 2001, p. 448.

9   Sasse, Gwendolyn, *The Crimea Question: Identity, Transition, and Conflict.* Cambridge, MA: Harvard University Press, 2007, pp. 137-138.

10 Kent, Neil and Yan Naumkin, 'Perception of the Cuban missile crisis in Russia Today' in *An International History of the Cuban Missile Crisis: A 50-year retrospective* David Gioe, Lenn Scott and Christopher Andrew, (eds.). New York: Routledge 2014, pp. 279-286.

11 Sasse, p. 225.

12 Glyn Williams, Brian, *The Crimean Tatars: The Diaspora Experience and the Forging of a Nation.* (Leiden, Boston and Köln, 2001) pp. 448-454.

13 Open Society Institute, *Crimean Tatars: Repatriation and Conflict Prevention.* New York: Open Society Institute, 1996, p. 79.

14 Sasse, p. 190.

15 Magocsi, p. 146.

16 Ibid.

17 Ayvazyan, Hovhannes M. (ed.), *The Armenia Diaspora Encyclopedia.* Yerevan: Haykakan Hanragitaran Publishing, 2003, p. 601.

18 Feodosia Office of Statistics.

EPILOGUE: CRIMEA IN THE TWENTY-FIRST CENTURY

1   Pew Research Centre, publication statistics issued on 8 May 2014.

BIBLIOGRAPHY

Acherson, Neal, *Black Sea: The Birthplace of Civilisation and Barbarism*. London: Vintage, 2007.

Akten zur Geschichte des Krimkriegs: Österreichische Akten zur Geschichte des Krimkriegs, ser. I, vol. 2 (Munich, 1980).

Ayvazyan, Hovhannes M. (ed.), *The Armenia Diaspora Encyclopedia*. Yerevan: Haykakan Hanragitaran Publishing, 2003.

Baumgart, Winifried, *The Crimean War, 1853-1856*. London: Hodder Education, 1999.

Bayley, C., *Mercenaries for the Crimean: The German, Swiss, and Italian Legions in British Service 1854-6*. Montreal, 1977.

Best, Geoffrey, *Humanity in Warfare: The Modern History of the International Law of Armed Conflicts*. London: Routledge, 1980.

Bitis, A., *Russia and the Eastern Question: Army, Government and Society 1815-1833*. Oxford: Oxford University Press, 2006.

Bykova, Tetiana B., *Stvorennia Kryms 'koi ASRR, 1917-1921*. Kiev: In-t istorii Ukrainy, 2011.

Chamberlain, M., *Lord Aberdeen: A Political Biography*. London: Longman, 1983.

Chorniy, Serhiy, *Natsionalny skald naselennia Ukraïny v XX storichchy: dovidnyk*. Kiev, 2011.

Cler, J., *Reminiscences of an Officer of Zouaves*. New York: D. Appleton, 1860.

de Damas, A., *Souvenirs Religieux et Militaires de la Crimée*. Paris: Jacques Lecoffre, 1857.

Diulichev, Valerii, *Krym: istoriia v ocherkakh-XX vet*. Simferopol, 2006.

Feodosia Office of Statistics.

Figes, Orlando, *The Crimean War: A History*. New York: Picador, 2010.

Fisher, Alan, *The Crimean Tatars*. Stanford, CA.: Hoover Institution Press 1978.

Foreign Office 181/114, Palmerston to Ponsonby, 6 Dec. 1833.

——— 78/413, Young to Palmerston, 29 Jan. and 28 Apr. 1840; 78/368, Young to Palmerston, 14 Mar. and 21 Oct. 1839.

Frank, J., *Dostoevsky: The Years of Ordeal, 1850-1859*. Princeton: Princeton University Press, 1983.

Gerbet, Klaus (ed.), *von Bock, Generalfeldmarschall Fedor: War Diary 1939-1945*. Atglen, PA: Schiffer, 1996.

Gleason, J., *The Genesis of Russophobia in Great Britain*. Cambridge, MA: Harvard University Press, 1950.

Gordon, Charles George, *General Gordon's Letters from the Crimea, the Danube and Armenia*. London, 1884.

Gökbilgin, Özalp (ed. and trans.), *Histoire de Sahip Giray, Khan de Crimée de 1532 à 1551*. Ankara, 1973.

Grigoriev, M.S. and O.F. Kovitidi, *Krym: istoria vozvrashenia*. Moscow, 2014.

Guerin, L., *Histoire de la Dernière Guerre de Russie (1853-1856)*, 2 vols. Paris: Dufour, Mulat, Boulanger, 1858, vol. 2.

Hawthorne, N., *The English Notebooks, 1853-1856*. Columbus, OH: Ohio State University Press, 1997.

Herbé, J., *Français et Russes en Crimée: Lettres d'un Officier Français à sa Famille pendant la Campagne d'Orient*. Paris, 1892.

Hodasevich, R., *A Voice from within the Walls of Sebastopol: A Narrative of the Campaign in the Crimea and the Events of the Siege*. London: John Murray, 1856.

Hornby, Lady E., *Constantinople during the Crimean War*. London: Bentley, 1863.

İnalcık, Halil, 'The Khan and the Tribal Aristocracy: The Crimean Khanate under Sahib Giray I' in *Harvard Ukrainian Studies*, 1979-80, 3-4.

Ivanics, Mária, 'The Military Co-operation of the Crimean Khanate with the Ottoman Empire in the Sixteenth and Seventeenth Centuries' in *The European Tributary States of the Ottoman Empire in the Sixteenth and Seventeenth Centuries*, Gábor Kármán and Lovro Kunçević (eds.). Leiden/Boston: Brill, 2013.

Journal of Refugee Studies Special Issue: The Odyssey of the Pontic Greeks, Vol, 4, No. 4. Oxford, 1991.

Kagan, Frederick W., *The Military Reforms of Nicholas I: The Origins of the Modern Russian Army*. London: Palgrave Macmillan, 1999.

Kent, Neil and Yan Naumkin, 'Perception of the Cuban missile crisis in Russia Today' in *An International History of the Cuban Missile Crisis: A 50-year retrospective* David Gioe, Lenn Scott and Christopher Andrew, (eds.). New York: Routledge 2014.

Kinross, Lord P., *Ottoman Centuries: The Rise and Fall of the Turkish Empire*. New York: Morrow Quill, 1977.

Knolles, Richard, *The Generall Historie of the Turkes*. London: Adam Islip, 1603.

Knollys, W., *The Victoria Cross in The Crimea: Deeds of Daring Library*. London: Dean & Son, 1877.

Koromila, Marianna (ed.), *Greeks in the Black Sea*. Athens, 1991.

Kozelsky, Mara, *Christianizing in the Russian Empire and Beyond*. De Kalb, IL.: Northern Illinois University Press, 2010.

Kozytskiy, Andriy, *Henotsyd ta polityka masovoho vynyshchennia tsyvil'noho naselennia u XX st*. Lviv, 2012.

Królikowska, Natalia, 'Sovereignty and Subordination in Crimean-Ottoman Relations (Sixteenth-Eighteenth Centuries)' in *The European Tributary States of the Ottoman Empire in the Sixteenth and Seventeenth Centuries*, Gábor Kármán and Lovro Kunçević (eds.). Leiden/Boston: Brill, 2013.

Kubijovyč, Volodymyr (ed.), *'Crimea' Encyclopedia of Ukraine*, Vol, I . Toronto, 1984.

Lettre du Prince Moustapha Fazil à Sa Majesté Abdul Aziz, Sultan de Turquie, 1866. Paris: Le Caire, 1940.

Lordkiparidze, R. (Head of the NKVD in Crimea), to the 18th Conference of the

Communist Party of the Crimean A.S.S.R., Diulichev, Valerii *Krym: istoriia v ocherkakh-XX vet.* Simferopol, 2006.

Magocsi, Paul Robert, *The Blessed Land: Crimea and the Crimean Tatars.* Toronto: Toronto University Press, 2014.

Maksoudian, Krikor, 'Armenian Communities in Eastern Europe' in *Armenian People From Ancient to Modern Times, Volume II: Foreign Dominion to Statehood: The Fifteenth Century to the Twentieth Century*, Richard G. Hovannisian, (ed.). New York: St. Martin's Press, 1997.

Marline, R., 'L'Opinion franc-comtoise deviant la guerre de Crimeé' in *Annales Littéraires de l'Université de Besançon*, vol. 17. Paris, 1957.

Margrave, R., 'Numbers & Losses in the Crimea: An Introduction'. *War Correspondent*, 21/1, 21/2, 21/3, 2003.

Masquelez, M., *Journal d'un Officier de Zouaves.* Paris, 1858.

Maude, A., *The Life of Tolstoy: First Fifty Years.* London: Constable, 1908.

Milner, Rev. T., *The Crimea: Its Ancient and Modern History*. London: Longman, Brown, Green, and Longmans, 1855.

Letter of A. Mokrousov and the secretary of the Simferopol Committee of the Communist party S. Martinov, dated July 1942, *Kozyts'kyi, Andrii Henotsyd ta polityka masovoho vynyshchennia tsyvil'noho naselennia u XX st.* L'viv, 2012.

Movsisyan, Jivan, 'The Tragedy of Crimean Armenians'. (Armenian) *Azg Daily,* Yerevan, 24 June 1998.

Murphy, David, *Ireland and the Crimean War.* Dublin: Four Courts Press, 2002.

Open Society Institute, *Crimean Tatars: Repatriation and Conflict Prevention.* New York: Open Society Institute, 1996

Pamuk, Şevket, *A Monetary History of the Ottoman Empire,* Cambridge: Cambridge University Press, 2005.

Penskoi, V.V., 'Voennyi potentsial Krymskogo Khanstva v konce XV-nachale XVII v.' *Vostok (Oriens)* [20], no. 2, 2010.

Pohl, J. Otto, *Ethnic Cleansing in the USSR: 1937-1949*, from the series Contributions to the Study of World History, Number 65. Westport, CN: Greenwood Press, 1999.

The Letters of Queen Victoria: A Selection from Her Majesty's Correspondence between the Years 1837 and 1861, 3 vols. London: John Murray, 1907-8, vol. 2.

Rappaport, H., *No Place for Ladies: The Untold Story of Women in the Crimean War.* London: Aurum Press, 2007.

Rieber, Alfred J., *The Struggle for the Eurasian Borderlands: From the Rise of Early Modern Empires to the End of the First World War.* Cambridge: Cambridge University Press, 2014.

Roberts, Andrew, *The Storm of War. A New History of the Second World War.* London: Penguin, 2009.

Rostovtzeff, M., *Iranians and Greeks in South Russia.* Oxford: Oxford University Press, 1989.

Russell, William Howard, *The Times,* 28 May 1855.

St Aubyn, G., *Queen Victoria: A Portrait.* London: Atheneum Books 1991.

Sasse, Gwendolyn, *The Crimea Question: Identity, Transition, and Conflict*. Cambridge, MA: Harvard University Press, 2007.

Schiemann, T., *Geschichte Russlands unter Kaiser Nikolaus I*, 4 vols. Berlin, 1904-19, vol. 4.

Schroeder, P., *Austria, Great Britain and the Crimean War: The Destruction of the European Concert*. New York: Cornell University Press, 1972.

Sebag Montefiore, Simon, *Prince of Princes: The Life of Potemkin*. London: Weidenfeld and Nicholson, 2000.

Sheehy, Anne, 'The Crimean Tatars and Volga Germans: Soviet Treatment of Two National Minorities' in *Minority Rights Group Report*, No. 6. London, 1971.

Small, H., *The Crimean War: Queen Victoria's War with the Russian Tsars*. Stroud: The History Press, 2007.

Smiley, Will, '"After being so long Prisoners, they will not return to Slavery in Russia": An Aegean Network of Violence between Empires and Identities' in *Osmanlı Araştırmaları / The Journal of Ottoman Studies*, XLIV, 2014.

Smirnov, V. D., *Krimskoy Hanstvo XIII–XV vv*. Moscow, 2011.

Struve, Joseph C. von (anon.), *Travels in the Crimea: A History of the Embassy from Petersburg to Constantinople in 1793*. London, 1802.

Tarle, E., *Krymskaia voina*, vol. 1. Moscow, 1944.

Taylor, Timothy, 'The Gundestrup Cauldron', *Scientific American*, March 1992.

———— 'Tracians, Scythians and Dacians', *Oxford Illustrated Prehistory of Europe*. Oxford: Oxford University Press, 1994.

———— 'Scythian and Armatian Art' *Dictionary of Art*. London, Macmillan, 1996.

Taylor, Timothy and T. Sulimirski, 'The Scythians', *Cambridge Ancient History*, 2nd edn., 1991.

Tolstoy, Leo, *Sebastopol Sketches*, D. McDuff (trans.). London: Penguin, 1986.

Tomsinov, V. A., '"Crimean law" or legal basis for the reunification of Crimea with Russia' *Vestnik Moscovskovo universiteta*. Seria 11 'Pravo', 2014.

Verney, H., Our Quarrel with Russia (London 1855), pp. 22–24.

Vitzthum von Eckstadt, K., *St Petersburg and London in the Years 1852-64*, 2 vols. London, 1887, vol I.

Williams, Brian Glyn, *The Crimean Tatars: The Diaspora Experience and the Forging of a Nation*. Leiden, Boston and Köln: Brill, 2001.

CHRONOLOGY OF POLITICAL, SOCIAL AND CULTURAL EVENTS IN CRIMEA

8TH AND 7TH CENTURY BC: Arrival of the Cimmerians, followed by the Scythians.

6TH CENTURY BC: Greeks establish themselves at Chersonesus, Theodoro and Panticapaeum (Bospor).

6–5TH CENTURY BC: Arrival of Taurians; construction of stone dolmens.

5TH CENTURY BC: Political zenith of the Scythians.

513 BC: Invasion of Persian King Darius the Great repelled.

C. 480 BC: Greek colonies in Crimea and Taman region combine into Bosporan state.

389–348BC: King Levon I expands the Bosporan Kingdom.

339 BC: King Ateas of the Scythians falls in battle against King Philip II of Macedonia.

3RD CENTURY BC: Arrival of the Sarmatians, who included Alans and Roxolani.

124–113 BC: Reign of Scythian King Skilurus, final flowering of Scythian Kingdom.

2ND CENTURY BC: Final collapse of Scythian kingdom under last King Palakus.

110 BC: Panticapaeum (Bospor) conquered by King Mithradates VI Eupator.

44–14 BC: Mithradates VI Eupator's granddaughter, Dynamis, appointed its first reigning queen.

MID 3RD CENTURY AD: Goths arrive in Crimea, capturing Neapolis (Simferopol).

350–375 AD: Zenith of Ostrogothic Kingdom, under Ermanaric.

527–565 AD: Zenith of Byzantine rule under Emperor Justinian I.

988: Prince Vladimir of Kiev baptised into Byzantine Orthodoxy at Chersonesus.

MID 11TH CENTURY: Arrival of the Armenians many of whom settle at Kaffa (Feodosia).

1100s: Arrival of Karaite Tatars in Crimea.

1296: Venetian fleet attacks Genoese at Kaffa.

1222: Mongols invade Crimea.

1280s: Foundation of Genoese colony at Kaffa.

1338: Crimea subdued by Batu Khan, grandson of Genghis Khan, founder of the Golden Horde.

1347–48: Visitation of the Black Death, which spreads further throughout Europe.

14TH CENTURY: Construction of Armenian Church of St Sarkis (Sergey), in Feodosia; Mangup capital of the Principality of Theodoro.

14–15TH CENTURY: Construction of the Genoese Fortress of Sydak.

EARLY 15TH CENTURY: Mausoleum of Golden Horde princess Janike.

1441: Establishment of Crimean Tatar Khanate, independent of the Golden Horde, under the Giray dynasty, under Haci Giray.

1475: Fall of Mangup–Theodoros, Kaffa, Tana, etc. to Ottoman Turks and Tatars.

1476: Crimean Tatar troops assist Dustan Mehmed II's forces in Moldavia.

1500: Venetian architect Aleviz (Aloisio) builds the first palace of Bakhchisaray for Khan Mengli–Giray.

1514: Crimean Tatars assist the Ottomans in defeating the Persians at Chaldiran and Tebriz.

1521: Crimean Tatars attack and pillage Moscow.

1571: Crimean Tatars again attack Moscow.

1572: Khan Devlet I Giray defeated by Moscow at the Battle of Molodi.

1579: Polish emissary Marcin Brqniewski visits Khan Mehmet Giray and eventually publishes his memoirs Marcopia on the visit.

1591: Khan Kazy-Giray makes devastating forays into Russia.

1648: Zaporozhian Cossacks briefly ally themselves with the Crimean Tatars against the Polish-Lithuanian Commonwealth.

1664: Until this year up to a million Slavs had been carried off into slavery by the Crimean Tatars since their arrival in the region.

1703–10: Ottoman Turks build the Fortress of Yenikale, near Kerch.

1704: Chronicle of Khan Mehmet Giray sheds light on Crimean subordination to the Ottomans.

1711: Ottomans fail to support Crimea against Russia.

1736: General Field Marshall Count von Münnich overruns Ottoman defences in Crimea, destroying the old palace of Bakhchisary.

1768–74: Russian-Ottoman War which ends in the Treaty of Küçük Kaynarca, which gives Russia the Ottoman fortresses of Yenikale and Kerch.

1771: Sahin Giray, heir apparent to the throne of the Crimean Khan, visits the court in St Petersburg of Catherine the Great.

1783: Russian-Ottoman Treaty of Ainalikawak, Russian annexation of Crimea; Sevastopol established as the site of a new Russian naval base.

1785: Crimean Tatar nobles granted patents of Russian nobility and tax privileges.

1787: Russian Empress Catherine the Great and Austrian Emperor Joseph II visit Crimea.

1792: Treaty of Jassi (now Iasi) ends new Russian-Ottoman war.

1794: Establishment of Muslim administrative body in Crimea.

1798: Russian poet Gavrila Derzhavin publishes his poem *The Waterfall*, glorifying Potemkin as the conquerer of New Russia and its Crimean province of Taurida.

1823: Count Mikhail Semyon Vorontsov appointed governor of New Russia, including Taurida Province, to which Crimea belonged. Russian poet Alexander Pushkin publishes his poem *The Fountain of Bakhchisaray* about unrequited love in the old Crimean Tatar capital.

1826: Polish poet Alexander Mickiewicz published eighteeen Crimean Sonnets.

1826–1837: Construction of the Naryshkin palace by the British architect Philip Elson.

1827: Archaeological excavations carried out at Khersonesos.

1828–29: Renewed Russian-Ottoman War.

1828–1848: Construction of Vorontsov's Alupka Palace by British architect Edward Blore.

1837: Tsar Nicholas I and family visit Alupka.

1842–52: Oreanda Palace built for Nicholas I (burnt down 1882).

1850: Ecclesiastical initiative of Russian Orthodox Archbishop Innokenty to restore and expand Crimean monasteries and churches.

1853: Russian refusal to accept the Four Points Ultimatum demanded by Britain, France and the Ottoman Empire.

1854: Crimean War breaks out on 28 March between Britain, France and the Ottoman Empire, on one side, Russia, on the other.

   Allies land at Yevpatoria 14 September.

   Battle of the Alma 20 September.

   First assault on Sevastopol 17–19 October.

   Battle of Balaclava 25 October.

   Battle of Inkerman 5 November.

   British nurse Florence Nightingale arrives at Scutari.

1855: Sardinia enters war against Russia 26 January.

1855: Tsar Nicholas II dies 2 March; he is succeeded by his eldest son Alexander II.

8 September, Malakov Tower taken by the French. Russians flee Sevastopol.

1856: Crimean War draws to a close with the defeat of Russia; peace concluded by the Treaty of Paris 30 March; over 750,000 men had lost their lives.

1861–92: Reconstruction of St Vladimir's Cathedral at Chersonesus.

1874: Universal conscription introduced in Russia.

1881–82 AND 1892–1902: Construction of the imperial Massandra Palace by the architects Étienne Bouchard and Maximilian Messmacher.

1883: Crimean Tatar newspaper *Tercuman* (*Interpreter*), established; it was published until 1914.

1888–92: Construction of the Resurrection Cathedral at Foros by Russian architect Nikolai Chagin.

1900: Russian poet Ivan Bunin publishes his nostalgic Crimean poem, *Long alley leading down to the shore*.

1903: Armenian composer Alexander Spendiaryan publishes his symphonic *Crimean Sketches*.

1906–7: Establishment of first Crimean Tatar women's movement periodical *Women's World*.

1907: Crimean Tatar Nurlu Kabirler-Abdürreşid Mehdi takes his seat in the Russian Duma in St Petersburg.

1909: Secret Homeland organisation established to encourage independence for Crimea under the Tatars.

1910–11: Construction of the Livadia Palace for Tsar Nicholas II and his family by Russian architect Nikolay Krasnov.

1914: Outbreak of the First World War; Sevastopol and Feodosia bombarded in October.

1917: Outbreak of the Russian Revolution and convocation of an All Crimean Muslim Conference in March and in late autumn a Crimean Tatar National Assembly at Bakhchisaray. Establishment of the Bolshevik Sevastopol Soviet.

1918: Crimean Regional Government established under General Sulkiewicz, support by the Germans; it collapses with their departure at the end of the year. Arrival of White General Deniken.

1919: Crimean Soviet Socialist Republic proclaimed on 29 April under Dimitry Ulyanov, Lenin's brother.

1920: Baron Wrangel musters White troops in Crimea until November; 144,000 refugees flee by ship. Béla Kun and the Bolshevik Terror briefly reign.

1921: Establishment of the Crimean Autonomous Socialist Soviet Republic on 21 October and the rehabilitation of many Crimean Tatars initiated; severe drought afflicts Crimea, creating a famine which leads to the death of over a 100,000 inhabitants.

1931–35: Houses of worship closed in Crimea and the clergy were either murdered or deported.

1935–37: Purges and deportations in Crimea.

1941: German 11th Army, under General Field Marshal Gerd von Rundstedt, invades Crimea in September; shortly thereafter, the annihilation of the Jews is undertaken – Crimea is declared 'free of Jews' in April 1942.

1942: German army celebrates the fall of Sevastopol in the Livadia Palace in July; Crimea is annexed to the Reichskomissariat Ukraine as the Generalbezirk Krim and became an important testing ground for Aryanisation and German resettlement by the Nazi regime; Tatars are wooed by the Germans and thousands volunteer to join them. A minority remains loyal to the Soviet Union.

1943: Defeat at the Battle of Stalingrad leads to the collapse of the German occupation.

1944: Soviet forces recapture Crimea in late spring. Deportation of some 220,000 Crimean Tatars, most to Soviet central Asia, follows. Further deportations of Armenians, Bulgarians and Greeks follows.

1945: Crimean Conference, which met at Yalta from 4–11 February, in which US president Franklin D. Roosevelt, British prime minister Winston

Churchill and Soviet leader Joseph Stalin, come to an arrangement over the defeat of Nazi Germany and the post-war settlement organised according to spheres of influence for the victors. On 30 June, Crimea becomes an *oblast* (region) within the Russian Soviet Federate Social Republic of the Soviet Union.

1949: Deportation of the Greeks.

1954: Crimea ceded to Ukraine from Russia by order of Russian Premier Nikita Khrushchev.

1956–57: Rehabilitation – but not resettlement – of the Crimean Tatars begins.

1962: Cuban Missile Crisis gives renewed importance to the Russian naval base at Sevastopol.

1968: Crimean Tatars petition, but without success, for their return to Crimea; some return to their homeland illegally, only a minority of whom are allowed to stay.

1975: Crimea's iron ore industry is so successful that it produces 39 times its pre-war level; other industries also achieve remarkable success, including agriculture and food processing. Russian tourism and sanatoria flourish.

1987: Crimean Tatar demonstration is permitted in Moscow's Red Square.

1989: Crimean Tatars are finally granted the right to return to their homeland; some 135,000 then return. Other ethnic minorities also return in significant numbers.

1991: After a referendum in which 93 per cent support the idea, Crimea is re-established as the Crimean Soviet Socialist Republic, within the Soviet Union. This is then overruled by the government of a now independent Ukraine, which declares Crimea an autonomous republic within Soviet Ukraine.

1995: Ukrainian government abolishes the office of the president of Crimea and the validity of any Crimean constitutions.

1997: Russia and Ukraine sign a Treaty of Friendship which renews Russia's lease over Sevastopol and its naval base until 2017; St Vladimir's

Cathedral, at Khersonesus is rebuilt under the patronage of President
Kuchma of Ukraine and President Putin of the Russia.

2005: International Festival of the Karaites held in Yevpatoria.

2010: Russia renews its agreement with Ukraine over Sevastopol and its
naval base until 2042.

2014: Russian-held referendum on 16 March declares that most Crimeans
want the autonomous republic, together with separately administered
Sevastopol, to join the Russian Federation; the Russian government accede
to this 'request' and Crimea becomes a part of the Russian Federation,
wide-spread American and European disapproval notwithstanding.

INDEX

INDEX

INDEX

Bondurand, Alexis-Adolphebone
 tools, 6
Boris Gudonov, Regent of Russia, 43, 46
Borodino, Battle of (1812), 62
Bospor, Crimea, 12
Bosporus Kingdom (438 BC – 370 AD),
 13, 15
Bosporus Straits, 48
Bosquet, Pierre, 82
Botkin, Sergei, 115
Bouchard, Étienne, 113
bows and arrows, 11, 43
boyars, 66
Bramante, Donato, 64
Brandenburg, 39
Brezhnev, Leonid, 113, 143
bribery, 38
Brighton Pavilion, England, 63
British hotel, Kadikoi, 95
British Museum, London, 9
Broniewski, Marcin, 34
bronze helmets, 11
Brunov, Baron, 69
Bucharest, Romania, 79
Buckingham Palace, London, 63, 69
Buckinghamshire, England, 87
Buddhism, 47, 144
Bug River, 48, 51
Bulgaria, Bulgarians, 57, 92, 103, 106,
 120, 123, 138–9, 153
Bunin, Ivan, 63
Buran Kaya III, Crimea, 6
Byzantine Empire (c. 330–1453), 2, 14,
 16–17, 19, 20, 22, 24, 25, 26, 30, 34,
 55, 65, 71

Cameron, Charles, 63
Canada, 123
Canning, Stratford, 1st Viscount
 Stratford de Redcliffe, 101, 102

de Canrobert, François Certain, 85
cantinières, 94
Capita-n-Kara, 5
capitalism, 123, 128
Capitoline Museum, Rome, 11
caravansarai, 24, 25
Cardiatricon, Ayu Dagh, 60
Cardwell, Edward, 99
Carpathian Mountains, 2, 4
Carrara marble, 64
Caspian Sea, 24, 27
de Castellane, Boniface, 97
Castro, Fidel, 146
Cathedral of St Alexander Nevsky,
 Simferopol, 107
Cathedral of St Vladimir, Chersonesus,
 60, 85, 107
Cathedral of the Archangel Michael,
 Kremlin, 29
Catherine II the Great, Empress and
 Autocrat of All the Russias, 2, 48,
 51–2, 53, 55, 56, 63, 67, 85, 154
Catholic Armenian Church, 22, 70
Catholicism, 23, 25, 26, 29, 71, 72, 75,
 76, 92, 154
cattle, 1, 11
Caucasus, 4, 10, 14, 21, 31, 35, 37, 41,
 62, 69, 71, 75, 77, 78, 79, 88, 93,
 103, 131, 142, 153
Caucasus War (1817–64), 69, 75, 79,
 88, 93
Causeway Bridge, Lake Pontchartrain,
 161
cavalry, Crimean Tatar, 36–7, 42, 118
Cavour, Camillo, 105
Cembalo, Crimea, 21
Central Asia, 2, 71, 110, 137–8, 144
Central Rada, 119, 120
Chagin, Nikolai, 107, 108
chain mail, 11

188

INDEX

Chaldiran, Persia, 32
Chalkidiki Peninsula, Greece, 61
Challen, Albert Charles, 95
Champoiseau, Charles, 79
Charge of the Light Brigade, The
(Tennyson), 84
Charles, Marquis de La Valette, 72
Charlotte, Princess of Württemberg, 90
Chatyr-Dag, 4
Chechnya, 69, 79, 142, 153
Cheka, 122
Chekhov, Anton, 1, 64, 86, 150
Chekhova, Yevgenia, 86
Chelebi-Jihan, Noman, 111, 112, 118,
119, 120
chemical industry, 142
Chenery, Thomas, 91–2
Chenetsov, Nikanor, 66–7
Chernaia River, 96
Cherniaev, Mikhail, 103
Chersonesus, Crimea, 12, 16, 19, 60,
61, 85, 107, 149
China, 21, 24, 73, 89, 139
Chiswick House, London, 69
Chobanzade, Bekir, 124
Chodasiewicz, Robert, 82
Chornovil, Viacheslav, 144
Christianity, 14, 15, 16, 19, 20, 21, 22,
23, 25, 26, 29, 33, 34–5, 36, 37, 38,
39, 43, 45, 50, 51, 52, 53, 56, 57,
60–1, 64, 70, 71, 75, 76, 77–8, 81,
85, 91, 99, 101, 102, 103, 104, 105–
8, 111, 125, 149–50, 153, 154
Anglican Church, 76, 91; Armenian
Apostolic Church, 21, 22, 25, 35,
149; Bible, 76–7; Catholic
Armenian Church, 22, 70;
Catholicism, 23, 25, 26, 29, 71,
72, 75, 76, 92, 154; Church of
Scotland, 76; churches, 20, 21, 23,
60, 62, 65, 72, 83, 105, 107–8,
125, 149–50, 153; conversion,
61, 102; Devil, 83; Greek
Orthodox Church, 35, 51, 56, 101;
Lutheranism, 91; monasteries, 19,
61, 72, 106, 125, 149–50, 153;
Old Believers, 48; Russian
Orthodox Church, 16, 19–20, 23,
32, 35, 38, 41, 45, 47, 48, 52, 53,
60–1, 71–2, 75, 76, 81, 104,
105, 106, 111, 125, 149–50,
154; Trinitarians, 16; Ukrainian
Orthodox Church, 154
Chronicle of Mehmed Giray, 49
Chubarov, Refat, 159
Chufut-Kale, Crimea, 14, 25, 33–4, 50,
108
Church of Scotland, 76
Church of St Catherine, Feodosia, 108
Church of St John the Baptist, Kerch, 20
Church of St Vladimir, Chersonesus, 60,
85, 107
Church of the Exaltation of the Cross,
° Livadia Palace, 65
Church of the Holy Sepulchre,
Jerusalem, 71
Church of the Saviour on the Spilled
Blood, St Petersburg, 107
churches, 20, 21, 23, 60, 62, 65, 72, 83,
105, 107–8, 125, 149–50, 153
Churchill, Winston, 65, 139
Cimmerian stylistic school, 130
Cimmerians, 6, 9–10
Circassians, 31, 36, 79, 103
Cler, Jean, 85
climate, 88–9
Cold War, 142
collective farms, 4, 124, 127–8
Colt, Samuel, 74
communications, 80, 91–2, 162

INDEX

INDEX

INDEX

INDEX

INDEX

INDEX

INDEX

INDEX

INDEX

INDEX

INDEX

of St Alexander Nevsky in Simferopol
completed, 107; construction of
Massandra estate begins, 113
1882 Oreanda Palace destroyed by
fire, 64; death of Vorontsov, 107
1883 Ismail Bey Gaspirali launches
Tercuman newspaper, 110
1884 New Method school opened in
Bakhchisaray, 110
1888 Church of St Vladimir Equal to
the Apostles in Chersonesus
completed, 107; construction of
Resurrection Church in Foros begins,
108
1889 Alexander III acquires
Massandra estate, 5, 113
1892 construction of Resurrection
Church in Foros, Crimea, 107,
108; reconstruction of Cathedral of
St Vladimir in Chersonesus
completed, 107; construction of St
Alexander Nevsky Cathedral in Yalta,
108; construction of Holy Mother of
God the Protectress at Sevastopol
begins, 108; construction of Church
of St Catherine at Feodosia, 108;
Messmacher begins work on
Massandra estate, 113
1893 construction of St Nicholas the
Wonder Worker at Yevpatoria begins,
108; Tsarevich Nicholas visits Britain,
109
1894 death of Alexander III; Nicholas
II becomes Tsar, 64, 109, 113
1895 construction of Dulber Palace in
Crimea begins, 113
1899 construction of St Nicholas the
Wonder Worker at Yevpatoria
completed, 108; Hague Peace
Conference, 109

1902 Messmacher's extension of
Massandra estate completed, 113
1903 Spendiaryan publishes *Crimean
Sketches*, 115
1905 Russo-Japanese War, 139;
construction of Holy Mother of God
the Protectress at Sevastopol
completed, 108; establishment of
Duma, 112
1906 Shefka Hanim Gaspirali launches
Women's World, 110
1907 Hague Peace Conference, 109;
Nurlu Kabirler Abdürreşid Mehdi
takes seat in Duma, 112
1908 foundation of Tatar Student
Association, 111; construction of
Sokolyne lodge in Crimea begins, 113
1909 foundation of Tatar Fatherland
Society, 111, 112, 118; Shevki
Bektöre migrates to Crimea, 111;
construction of Yusopov Palace, 113,
129
1910 Gaspirali launches *Public School*,
110; construction of Sokolyne lodge
in Crimea completed, 113
1911 Nicholas II opens new Livadia
Palace in Crimea, 64; construction of
Swallow's Nest in begins, 114
1914 Battle of Odessa; Ottoman
bombardment of Sevastopol and
Feodosia, 117
1916 Maximilian Voloshin settles in
Koktebel, 129; Fedor Shaliapin,
Maxim Gorky and Stepan Skitalets
visit Crimea, 115
1917 February Revolution, 5, 64–5,
112, 113, 116, 118, 126; Fatherland
Society holds All Crimean Muslim
Conference, 118; death of Maksim
Bohdanovich in Yalta, 114; foundation

INDEX

INDEX

INDEX